WITH GOD YOU ARE NEVER ALONE

WITH GOD YOU ARE NEVER ALONE

The Great Papal Addresses

BENEDICT XVI

BLOOMSBURY CONTINUUM
LONDON • OXFORD • NEW YORK • NEW DELHI • SYDNEY

BLOOMSBURY CONTINUUM
Bloomsbury Publishing Plc
50 Bedford Square, London, WC1B 3DP, UK
29 Earlsfort Terrace, Dublin 2, Ireland

BLOOMSBURY, BLOOMSBURY CONTINUUM and the Diana logo are
trademarks of Bloomsbury Publishing Plc

First published in Great Britain 2023

ISBN: HB: 978-1-3994-1372-5; TPB: 978-1-3994-1371-8;
eBook: 978-1-3994-1370-1; ePDF: 978-1-3994-1369-5

2 4 6 8 10 9 7 5 3

Typeset by Deanta Global Publishing Services, Chennai, India
Printed and bound in the U.S.A. by Berryville Graphics Inc.,
Berryville, Virginia

To find out more about our authors and books visit www.bloomsbury.com
and sign up for our newsletters

Contents

Preface

As everyone knows, it is not only the writings of the late Pope Benedict published during his pontificate but also his speeches and homilies which are so rich in their content and so clear in their expression.

It is possible now to read the entire published works of Joseph Ratzinger, including those from before he was elected Pope. In doing so we are confronted with a huge sea which, thanks to the publication of his complete works (*Opera Omnia*), can be reflected on in depth. At the same time, the thought of Benedict XVI is very coherent, one might even say organic, in its essence and in its development.

In this collection of his great addresses, we have limited ourselves strictly to those delivered during his pontificate. It is the Pope himself who speaks. The addresses are extremely easy to follow and are expressed simply and without obfuscation. The selection of these ten addresses has been made for the greatest impact possible.

Looking at the Table of Contents, it is clear that the collection is confined to the Pope's greatest and most important speeches but also delivered to a very specific audience. They are not just 'writings', let alone magisterial documents taken from the vast archive. They are not long, and they are limited by their context. This does not prevent Pope Benedict from bearing in mind the world at large, nor indeed the lessons of history.

The speeches range from the one he delivered at his inauguration as Pope to another delivered to priests at a time of clerical crisis and another when he announced his resignation. They range thus in time from the start to the end of his Papacy. And it will be seen that the addresses were given in a large variety of places: from St Peter's Square to the youth festival in Cologne, the gates of Auschwitz-Birkenau, the German Reichstag in Berlin and, of particular interest to English-language readers, Westminster Hall in London, where he addressed the members of the House of Lords and the House of Commons. This is, of course, where Sir Thomas More was put on trial, which has its irony.

It will be noted that all these addresses were delivered in Europe, and this is not accidental. Pope Benedict may well be the last 'European'

Pope; he was deeply immersed in the history and culture of Europe. It is in this context that Pope Benedict points to what he considers to be the dramatic breakdown today of the relationship between faith and reason. In all this, we witness his passion for truth.

The voice of Benedict himself is unmistakable. And in each case Benedict himself checked and approved the exact text, from the first word to the last. The addresses chosen fall into two categories: those concerned directly with the life of the Church and those concerned with culture, politics and society in the modern world.

'The Church is alive! This is the great experience of our time,' wrote Benedict. 'I am profoundly moved by this fact.' Benedict's pontificate began and ended with this testimony – the vitality of the Church – and he had been entrusted with leading it. In spite of difficulties, the Church is alive because Christ is alive, is risen. The Church belongs to him, and he is its Good Shepherd, however tempestuous the seas may be. God shows to man that we can meet Christ, it is He who saves us. He saves us in the desert and in darkness and leads us to the light and the life. The first address in this book is to young people; Benedict urges them not to be afraid of Christ, who takes nothing from us and gives us everything. He echoes the words of

Pope John Paul II: 'Do not be afraid. Open your door to Christ and let Him in.'

It was only a few months after this that Benedict addressed the world gathering of youth in Cologne. He urged his audience to be like the Three Kings and travel along the path of the Church. And this means the Church with all its faults, its defects, but made up of sinners and saints. These are the real revolutionaries of history, the people who teach the language of God, a language not of power but of truth.

For the renewal of the Church in our time, Benedict points us to the texts of the Second Vatican Council ('Vatican II'). Remember that Benedict himself had been an active participant in that Council, as a theological expert. He emphasized that the fruits of the Council had to develop and not remain static. In this way he believed a dialogue would ensue between science and religion, the modern secular state and the Church with its distinctive understanding of humanity and the place of humankind in society, and also between the Church and the other great religions of the world.

Remember also that Benedict was a pope–theologian who argued for the place of Christian faith in modern contemporary culture, and this without forgetting for one minute the great

problems of heading up the modern Church –
not least in the coming to light of so many sexual
scandals among the clergy, most particularly
among the Catholic clergy. It was to these sad and
painful scandals that Benedict had to devote so
much of his energy. Of his many utterances on this
subject, many are included in this volume.

With the existence of evil and bitter malevolence
in the Church, Benedict understood their real
harm; however, these would never extinguish the
fruits of Christ or the fruits of His holiness. The
last address in this book, to the people of Ireland,
is devoted specifically to the importance of the way
of conversion and renewal.

Other chapters relate to the relationship between
faith and reason. These are directed to outsiders
more specifically, to those outside the Church.
At Auschwitz he addresses the question 'Where
was God in those days?' With humility he travels
the long and perilous road to try and answer that
question.

We have, he argues, to see that God is a God
of reason and a reason which is not neutral but
is exercised in love and which leads us to see evil
for what it is and to reject it. In the Regensburg
speech, in particular, Benedict talks of the meeting
of the faith of the Bible and the demands of Greek
philosophy, which continues up to the present day.

In his Paris address he examines the origins of the Western theological tradition from the Middle Ages, demonstrating that the fruits of this tradition depend entirely on the *quaerere Deum*, that the absence of God arises from Him himself and that the search for God is the basis of true culture.

In Westminster Hall, Benedict argued strongly that there must be a place for religion in the political process, for reason and faith have need of each other, if our modern society is to flourish. Again if modern democratic society is founded from moral principles drawn for a consensus only, its fragility will be self-evident. In this way, it becomes impossible to distinguish good from evil in modern society. If we are to consider exclusively a positive form of reason, it is clear that humankind has a nature that needs to respect and not manipulate our well-being because mankind did not create itself.

This is why Pope Benedict urges a return to objective reason, which manifests itself in nature, examined and known to the subjective reason of humankind. This emphasizes the responsibility of man face to face with God and the inviolable dignity of man, made in God's image.

Let us remember that Pope Benedict always taught that the mission of the Church remains to talk always of the humanity of Christ, the God of Jesus Christ, especially at a time when God seems to have disappeared to the edges of secular mankind. Remember again that his vision was that the fruits of Vatican II were the belief that we must re-establish links between the Church and the modern world. All this he believed to be necessary for the salvation of mankind, of the whole human family in the face of the dramatic absence of belief in our times.

This is the message which emerges with great strength from the pages of this book, from these the most important addresses of Benedict XVI.

Fr Federico Lombardi
President of the Ratzinger–Benedict Foundation
Vatican City

1

Christ Guides the Church

Mass, Imposition of the Pallium and Conferral of the Fisherman's Ring for the Beginning of the Petrine Ministry of the Bishop of Rome

HOMILY OF HIS HOLINESS
BENEDICT XVI
ST PETER'S SQUARE
SUNDAY, 24 APRIL 2005

Your Eminences,
My dear Brother Bishops and Priests,
Distinguished Authorities and Members of the
Diplomatic Corps,
Dear Brothers and Sisters,

During these days of great intensity, we have chanted the litany of the saints on three different occasions: at the funeral of our Holy Father John Paul II; as the Cardinals entered the Conclave; and again today, when we sang it with the response *Tu illum adiuva* – sustain the new successor of St Peter. On each occasion, in a particular way, I found great consolation in listening to this prayerful chant. How alone we all felt after the passing of John Paul II – the Pope who for over twenty-six years had been our shepherd and guide on our journey through life! He crossed the threshold of the next life, entering into the mystery of God. But he did not take this step alone. Those who believe are never alone – neither in life nor in death. At that moment, we could call upon the saints from every age – his friends, his brothers and sisters in the faith – knowing that they would form a living procession to accompany him into the next world, into the glory of God. We knew that his arrival was awaited. Now we know that he is among his own and is truly at home.

We were also consoled as we made our solemn entrance into Conclave, to elect the one whom the Lord had chosen. How would we be able to discern his name? How could 115 bishops, from every culture and every country, discover the one on whom the Lord wished to confer the mission of binding and loosing? Once again, we knew that we were not alone; we knew that we were surrounded, led and guided by the friends of God. And now, at this moment, weak servant of God that I am, I must assume this enormous task, which truly exceeds all human capacity. How can I do this? How will I be able to do it? All of you, my dear friends, have just invoked the entire host of saints, represented by some of the great names in the history of God's dealings with mankind. In this way, I too can say with renewed conviction: I am not alone. I do not have to carry alone what in truth I could never carry alone. All the saints of God are there to protect me, to sustain me and to carry me. And your prayers, my dear friends, your indulgence, your love, your faith and your hope accompany me.

Indeed, the communion of saints consists not only of the great men and women who went before us and whose names we know. All of us belong to the communion of saints, we who have been baptized in the name of the Father, and of the Son and of the Holy Spirit, we who draw life from the gift of Christ's body and blood, through which he transforms us and makes us like himself. Yes, the Church is alive – this is the wonderful experience of these days. During those sad days of the Pope's illness and death, it became wonderfully evident to us that the Church is alive. And the Church is young. She holds within herself the future of the world and therefore shows each of us the way towards the future. The Church is alive, and we are seeing it: we are experiencing the joy that the Risen Lord promised his followers. The Church is alive – she is alive because Christ is alive, because he is truly risen. In the suffering that we saw on the Holy Father's face in those days of Easter, we contemplated the mystery of Christ's Passion and we touched his wounds. But throughout these days we have also been able, in a profound sense, to touch the Risen One. We have been able to experience the joy that he promised, after a brief period of darkness, as the fruit of his resurrection.

The Church is alive – with these words, I greet with great joy and gratitude all of you gathered here, my venerable brother cardinals and bishops, my dear priests, deacons, church workers, catechists. I greet you, men and women religious, witnesses of the transfiguring presence of God. I greet you, members of the lay faithful, immersed in the great task of building up the Kingdom of God which spreads throughout the world, in every area of life. With great affection I also greet all those who have been reborn in the sacrament of baptism but are not yet in full communion with us; and you, my brothers and sisters of the Jewish people, to whom we are joined by a great shared spiritual heritage, one rooted in God's irrevocable promises. Finally, like a wave gathering force, my thoughts go out to all men and women of today, to believers and non-believers alike.

Dear friends! At this moment there is no need for me to present a programme of governance. I was able to give an indication of what I see as my task in my message of Wednesday 20 April, and there will be other opportunities to do so. My real programme of governance is not to do my own will, not to pursue my own ideas, but to listen, together with the whole Church, to the word and the will of the Lord, to be guided by Him, so that He himself will lead the Church at this hour of our history. Instead of putting forward a programme, I should simply like to comment on the two liturgical symbols which represent the inauguration of the Petrine ministry; both these symbols, moreover, reflect clearly what we heard proclaimed in today's readings.

The first symbol is the pallium, woven in pure wool, which will be placed on my shoulders. This ancient sign, which the bishops of Rome have worn since the fourth century, may be considered an image of the yoke of Christ, which the bishop of this city, the servant of the servants of God, takes upon his shoulders. God's yoke is God's will, which we accept. And this will does not weigh down on us, oppressing us and taking away our freedom. To know what God wants, to know where the path of life is found – this was Israel's joy, this was her great privilege. It is also our joy: God's will does not alienate us, it purifies us – even if this can be painful – and so it leads us to ourselves. In this way we serve not only him but the salvation of the whole world, of all history. The symbolism of the pallium is even more concrete: the lamb's wool is meant to represent the lost, sick or weak sheep which the shepherd places on his shoulders and carries to the waters of life. For the Fathers of the Church, the parable of the lost sheep, which the shepherd seeks in the desert, was an image of the mystery of Christ and the Church. The human race – every one of us – is the sheep lost in the desert which no longer knows the way. The Son of God will not let this happen; he cannot abandon humanity in so wretched a condition. He leaps to his feet and abandons the glory of heaven, in order to go in search of the sheep and pursue it, all the way to the Cross. He takes it upon his shoulders and carries our humanity; he carries us all – he is the good shepherd who lays down his life for the sheep.

What the pallium indicates first and foremost is that we are all carried by Christ. But at the same time it invites us to carry one another. Hence the pallium becomes a symbol of the shepherd's mission, of which the second reading and the Gospel speak. The pastor must be inspired by Christ's holy zeal: for him it is not a matter of indifference that so many people are living in the desert. And there are so many kinds of desert. There is the desert of poverty, the desert of hunger and thirst, the desert of abandonment, of loneliness, of destroyed love. There is the desert of God's darkness, the emptiness of souls no longer aware of their dignity or the goal of human life. The external deserts in the world are growing, because the internal deserts have become so vast. Therefore the earth's treasures no longer serve to build God's garden for all to live in, but they have been made to serve the powers of exploitation and destruction. The Church as a whole and all her pastors, like Christ, must set out to lead people out of the desert, towards the place of life, towards friendship with the Son of God, towards the One who gives us life, and life in abundance.

The symbol of the lamb also has a deeper meaning. In the Ancient Near East, it was customary for kings to style themselves shepherds of their people. This was an image of their power, a cynical image: to them their subjects were like sheep, which the shepherd could dispose of as he wished. When the shepherd of all humanity, the living God, himself became a lamb, he stood on the side of the lambs, with those who are downtrodden and killed. This is how he reveals himself to be the true shepherd: 'I am the Good Shepherd ... I lay down my life for the sheep,' Jesus says of himself (Jn 10.14–15). It is not power but love that redeems us! This is God's sign: he himself is love. How often we wish that God would show himself to be stronger, that he would strike decisively, defeating evil and creating a better world. All ideologies of power justify themselves in exactly this way: they justify the destruction of whatever would stand in the way of progress and the liberation of humanity. We suffer on account of God's patience. And yet we need his patience. God, who became a lamb, tells us that the world is saved by the Crucified One, not by those who crucified him. The world is redeemed by the patience of God. It is destroyed by the impatience of man.

One of the basic characteristics of a shepherd must be to love the people entrusted to him, even as he loves Christ whom he serves. 'Feed my sheep,' says Christ to Peter, and now, at this moment, he says it to me as well. Feeding means loving, and loving also means being ready to suffer. Loving means giving the sheep what is truly good, the nourishment of God's truth, of God's word, the nourishment of his presence, which he gives us in the Blessed Sacrament. My dear friends – at this moment I can only say: pray for me, that I may learn to love the Lord more and more. Pray for me, that I may learn to love his flock more and more – in other words, you, the holy Church, each one of you and all of you together. Pray for me, that I may not flee for fear of the wolves. Let us pray for one another, that the Lord will carry us and that we will learn to carry one another.

The second symbol used in today's liturgy to express the inauguration of the Petrine ministry is the presentation of the fisherman's ring. Peter's call to be a shepherd, which we heard in the Gospel, comes after the account of a miraculous catch of fish: after a night in which the disciples had let down their nets without success, they see the Risen Lord on the shore. He tells them to let down their nets once more, and the nets become so full that they can hardly pull them in: 153 large fish, 'and although there were so many, the net was not torn' (Jn 21.11). This account, coming at the end of Jesus' earthly journey with his disciples, corresponds to an account found at the beginning: there too, the disciples had caught nothing the entire night; there too, Jesus had invited Simon once more to put out into the deep.

And Simon, who was not yet called Peter, gave the wonderful reply: 'Master, at your word I will let down the nets.' And then came the conferral of his mission: 'Do not be afraid. Henceforth you will be catching men' (Lk. 5.1–11). Today too the Church and the successors of the Apostles are told to put out into the deep sea of history and to let down the nets, so as to win men and women over to the Gospel – to God, to Christ, to true life. The Fathers made a very significant commentary on this singular task. This is what they say: for a fish, created for water, it is fatal to be taken out of the sea, to be removed from its vital element to serve as human food. But in the mission of a fisher of men, the reverse is true. We are living in alienation, in the salt waters of suffering and death, in a sea of darkness without light. The net of the Gospel pulls us out of the waters of death and brings us into the splendour of God's light, into true life. It is really true: as we follow Christ in this mission to be fishers of men, we must bring men and women out of the sea that is salted with so many forms of alienation and onto the land of life, into the light of God. It is really so: the purpose of our lives is to reveal God to men. And only where God is seen does life truly begin. Only when we meet the living God in Christ do we know what life is. We are not some casual and meaningless product of evolution. Each of us is the result of a thought of God. Each of us is willed; each of us is loved; each of us is necessary. There is nothing more beautiful than to be surprised by the Gospel, by the encounter with Christ. There is nothing more beautiful than to know Him and to speak to others of our friendship with Him. The task of the shepherd, the task of the fisher of men, can often seem wearisome. But it is beautiful and wonderful, because it is truly a service to joy, to God's joy, which longs to break into the world.

Here I want to add something: both the image of the shepherd and that of the fisherman issue an explicit call to unity. 'I have other sheep that are not of this fold; I must lead them too, and they will heed my voice. So there shall be one flock, one shepherd' (Jn 10.16); these are the words of Jesus at the end of his discourse on the Good Shepherd. And the account of the 153 large fish ends with the joyful statement: 'although there were so many, the net was not torn' (Jn 21.11). Alas, beloved Lord, with sorrow we must now acknowledge that it has been torn! But no – we must not be sad! Let us rejoice because of your promise, which does not disappoint, and let us do all we can to pursue the path towards the unity you have promised. Let us remember it in our prayer to the Lord, as we plead with him: yes, Lord, remember your promise. Grant that we may be one flock and one shepherd! Do not allow your net to be torn, help us to be servants of unity!

At this point, my mind goes back to 22 October 1978, when Pope John Paul II began his ministry here in St Peter's Square. His words on that occasion constantly echo in my ears: 'Do not be afraid! Open wide the doors for Christ!' The Pope was addressing the mighty, the powerful of this world, who feared that Christ might take away something of their power if they were to let him in, if they were to allow the faith to be free. Yes, he would certainly have taken something away from them: the dominion of corruption, the manipulation of law and the freedom to do as they pleased. But he would not have taken away anything that pertains to human freedom or dignity, or to the building of a just society. The Pope was also speaking to everyone, especially the young. Are we not perhaps all afraid in some way? If we let Christ enter fully into our lives, if we open ourselves totally to him, are we not afraid that He might take something away from us? Are we not perhaps afraid to give up something significant, something unique, something that makes life so beautiful? Do we not then risk ending up diminished and deprived of our freedom? And once again the Pope said: No!

If we let Christ into our lives, we lose nothing, nothing, absolutely nothing of what makes life free, beautiful and great. No! Only in this friendship are the doors of life opened wide. Only in this friendship is the great potential of human existence truly revealed. Only in this friendship do we experience beauty and liberation. And so today, with great strength and great conviction, on the basis of long personal experience of life, I say to you, dear young people: do not be afraid of Christ! He takes nothing away, and he gives you everything. When we give ourselves to him, we receive a hundredfold in return. Yes, open, open wide the doors to Christ – and you will find true life. Amen.

2

The Second Vatican Council: A Force to Renew the Church

*Address of His Holiness Benedict XVI
to the Roman Curia, Offering Them His
Christmas Greetings*

THURSDAY, 22 DECEMBER 2005

Your Eminences,
Venerable Brothers in the Episcopate and in the
Presbyterate,
Dear Brothers and Sisters,

'*Expergiscere, homo: quia pro te Deus factus est homo*
– Wake up, O man! For your sake God became
man' (St Augustine, *Sermon* 185). With the

Christmas celebrations now at hand, I am opening my meeting with you, dear collaborators of the Roman Curia, with St Augustine's invitation to understand the true meaning of Christ's birth.

I address to each one of you my most cordial greeting and I thank you for the sentiments of devotion and affection, effectively conveyed to me by your Cardinal Dean, to whom I address my gratitude.

God became man for our sake: this is the message which, every year, from the silent grotto of Bethlehem spreads even to the most out-of-the-way corners of the earth. Christmas is a feast of light and peace; it is a day of inner wonder and joy that expands throughout the universe, because 'God became man.' From the humble grotto of Bethlehem, the eternal Son of God, who became a tiny Child, addresses each one of us: he calls us, invites us to be reborn in him so that, with him, we may live eternally in communion with the most Holy Trinity.

Our hearts brimming with the joy that comes from this knowledge, let us think back to the events of the year that is coming to an end. We have behind us great events which have left a deep mark on the life of the Church. I am thinking, first and foremost, of the departure of our beloved Holy Father, John Paul II, preceded by a long period of suffering and the gradual loss of speech. No Pope has left us such a quantity of texts as he has bequeathed to us; no previous Pope was able to visit the whole world like him and speak directly to people from all the continents.

In the end, however, his lot was a journey of suffering and silence. Unforgettable for us are the images of Palm Sunday, when, holding an olive branch and marked by pain, he came to the window and imparted the Lord's Blessing as he himself was about to walk towards the Cross.

Next was the scene in his private chapel when, holding the crucifix, he took part in the Way of the Cross at the Colosseum, where he had so often led the procession carrying the Cross himself.

Lastly came his silent blessing on Easter Sunday, in which we saw the promise of the Resurrection, of eternal life, shine out through all his suffering. With his words and actions, the Holy Father gave us great things; equally important is the lesson he imparted to us from the chair of suffering and silence.

In his last book, *Memory and Identity*, he has left us an interpretation of suffering that is not a theological or philosophical theory but a fruit that matured on his personal path of suffering which he walked, sustained by faith in the Crucified Lord. This interpretation, which he worked out in faith and which gave meaning to his suffering lived in communion with that of the Lord, spoke through his silent pain, transforming it into an important message.

Both at the beginning and once again at the end of the book mentioned, the Pope shows that he is deeply touched by the spectacle of the power of evil, which we dramatically experienced in the century that has just ended. He says in his text: 'The evil … was not a small-scale evil. … It was an evil of gigantic proportions, an evil which availed itself of state structures in order to accomplish its wicked work, an evil built up into a system.'[1]

Might evil be invincible? Is it the ultimate power of history? Because of the experience of evil, for Pope Wojtyła the question of redemption became the essential and central question of his life and thought as a Christian. Is there a limit against which the power of evil shatters? 'Yes, there is,' the Pope replies in this book of his, as well as in his encyclical on redemption.

The power that imposes a limit on evil is Divine Mercy. Violence, the display of evil, is opposed in history – as 'the totally other' of God, God's own power – by Divine Mercy. The Lamb is stronger than the dragon, we could say together with the Book of Revelation.

At the end of the book, in a retrospective review of the attack of 13 May 1981 and on the basis of the experience of his journey with God and with the world, John Paul II further deepened this answer.

What limits the force of evil, the power, in brief, which overcomes it – this is how he puts it – is God's suffering, the suffering of the Son of God on the Cross:

> The suffering of the Crucified God is not just one form of suffering alongside others. ... In sacrificing himself for us all, Christ gave a new meaning to suffering, opening up a new dimension, a new order: the order of love. ... The passion of Christ on the Cross gave a radically new meaning to suffering, transforming it from within. ... It is this suffering which burns and consumes evil with the flame of love. ... All human suffering, all pain, all infirmity contains within itself a promise of salvation; ... evil is present in the world partly so as to awaken our love, our self-gift in generous and disinterested service to those visited by suffering. ... Christ has redeemed the world: 'By his wounds we are healed' (Is. 53.5).[2]

All this is not merely learned theology but the expression of a faith lived and matured through suffering. Of course, we must do all we can to alleviate suffering and prevent the injustice that causes the suffering of the innocent. However, we must also do our utmost to ensure that people can discover the meaning of suffering and are thus able to accept their own suffering and to unite it with the suffering of Christ.

In this way, it is merged with redemptive love and consequently becomes a force against the evil in the world.

The response across the world to the Pope's death was an overwhelming demonstration of gratitude for the fact that in his ministry he offered himself totally to God for the world, a thanksgiving for the fact that in a world full of hatred and violence he taught a new love and suffering in the service of others; he showed us, so to speak, in the flesh, the Redeemer, redemption, and gave us the certainty that indeed evil does not have the last word in the world.

I would now like to mention, albeit briefly, another two events also initiated by Pope John Paul II: they are the World Youth Day, celebrated in Cologne, and the Synod of Bishops on the Eucharist, which also ended the Year of the Eucharist, inaugurated by Pope John Paul II.

The World Youth Day has lived on as a great gift in the memory of those present. More than a million young people gathered in the city of Cologne on the River Rhine and in the neighbouring towns to listen together to the Word of God, to pray together, to receive the sacraments of Reconciliation and the Eucharist, to sing and to celebrate together, to rejoice in life and to worship and receive the Lord in the Eucharist during the great meetings on Saturday evening and Sunday. Joy simply reigned throughout those days.

Apart from keeping order, the police had nothing to do: the Lord had gathered his family, tangibly overcoming every frontier and barrier, and in the great communion between us he made us experience his presence.

The motto chosen for those days – 'We have come to worship him!' – contained two great images which encouraged the right approach from the outset. First there was the image of the pilgrimage, the image of the person who, looking beyond his own affairs and daily life, sets out in search of his essential destination, the truth, the right life, God.

This image of the person on his way towards the goal of life contained another two clear indications. First of all, there was the invitation not to see the world that surrounds us solely as raw material with which we can do something, but to try to discover in it 'the Creator's handwriting', the creative reason and the love from which the world was born and of which the universe speaks to us, if we pay attention, if our inner senses awaken and acquire perception of the deepest dimensions of reality.

As a second element there is a further invitation: to listen to the historical revelation which alone can offer us the key to the interpretation of the silent mystery of creation, pointing out to us the practical way towards the true Lord of the world and of history, who conceals himself in the poverty of the stable in Bethlehem.

The other image contained in the World Youth Day motto was that of the person worshipping: 'We have come to worship him.' Before any activity, before the world can change, there must be worship. Worship alone sets us truly free; worship alone gives us the criteria for our action. Precisely in a world in which guiding criteria are absent and the threat exists that each person will be a law unto himself, it is fundamentally necessary to stress worship.

For all those who were present the intense silence of that million young people remains unforgettable, a silence that united and uplifted us all when the Lord in the Blessed Sacrament was placed on the altar. Let us cherish in our hearts the images of Cologne: they are signs that continue to be valid. Without mentioning individual names, I would like on this occasion to thank everyone who made World Youth Day possible; but especially, let us together thank the Lord, for indeed, he alone could give us those days in the way in which we lived them.

The word 'adoration' (worship) brings us to the second great event that I wish to talk about: the Synod of Bishops and the Year of the Eucharist. Pope John Paul II, with the encyclical *Ecclesia de Eucharistia* and the apostolic letter *Mane Nobiscum Domine,* gave us the essential clues and at the same time, with his personal experience of Eucharistic faith, put the Church's teaching into practice.

Moreover, the Congregation for Divine Worship, in close connection with the encyclical, published the instruction *Redemptionis Sacramentum* as a practical guide to the correct implementation of the conciliar constitution on the liturgy and liturgical reform. In addition to all this, was it really possible to say anything new, to develop further the whole of this teaching?

This was exactly the great experience of the Synod, during which a reflection of the riches of the Eucharistic life of the Church today and the inexhaustibility of her Eucharistic faith could be perceived in the Fathers' contributions. What the Fathers thought and expressed must be presented, in close connection with the *Propositiones* of the Synod, in a post-Synodal document.

Here, once again, I only wish to underline that point which a little while ago we already mentioned in the context of World Youth Day: adoration of the Risen Lord, present in the Eucharist with flesh and blood, with body and soul, with divinity and humanity.

It is moving for me to see how everywhere in the Church the joy of Eucharistic adoration is reawakening and being fruitful. In the period of liturgical reform, Mass and adoration outside it were often seen as in opposition to one another: it was thought that the Eucharistic bread had been given to us not to be contemplated but to be eaten, as a widespread objection claimed at that time.

The experience of the prayer of the Church has already shown how nonsensical this antithesis was. Augustine had formerly said, '*nemo autem illam carnem manducat, nisi prius adoraverit; ... peccemus non adorando*' ('No one should eat this flesh without first adoring it; ... we should sin were we not to adore it') (cf. Ps. 98.9).

Indeed, we do not merely receive something in the Eucharist. It is the encounter and unification of persons; the person, however, who comes to meet us and desires to unite himself to us is the Son of God. Such unification can only be brought about by means of adoration.

Receiving the Eucharist means adoring the One whom we receive. Precisely in this way and only in this way do we become one with him. Therefore, the development of Eucharistic adoration, as it took shape during the Middle Ages, was the most consistent consequence of the Eucharistic mystery itself: only in adoration can profound and true acceptance develop. And it is precisely this personal act of encounter with the Lord that develops the social mission which is contained in the Eucharist and desires to break down barriers: not only the barriers between the Lord and us but also, and above all, those that separate us from one another.

The last event of this year on which I wish to reflect here is the celebration of the conclusion of the Second Vatican Council 40 years ago. This memory prompts the question of what has been the result of the Council. Was it well received? What, in the acceptance of the Council, was good and what was inadequate or mistaken? What still remains to be done? No one can deny that in vast areas of the Church the implementation of the Council has been somewhat difficult, even without wishing to apply to what occurred in these years the description that St Basil, the great Doctor of the Church, made of the Church's situation after the Council of Nicaea. He compares her situation to a naval battle in the darkness of the storm, saying among other things: 'The raucous shouting of those who through disagreement rise up against one another, the incomprehensible chatter, the confused din of uninterrupted clamouring, has now filled almost the whole of the Church, falsifying through excess or failure the right doctrine of the faith' (*De Spiritu Sancto, XXX, 77*).

We do not want to apply precisely this dramatic description to the situation of the post-Conciliar period, yet something from all that occurred is nevertheless reflected in it. The question arises of why has the implementation of the Council, in large parts of the Church, thus far been so difficult.

Well, it all depends on the correct interpretation of the Council or, as we would say today, on its proper hermeneutics, the correct key to its interpretation and application. The problems in its implementation arose from the fact that two contrary hermeneutics came face to face and quarrelled with each other. One caused confusion; the other, silently but more and more visibly, bore and is bearing fruit.

On the one hand, there is an interpretation that I would call 'a hermeneutic of discontinuity and rupture'; it has frequently availed itself of the sympathies of the mass media, and also one trend of modern theology. On the other, there is the 'hermeneutic of reform', of renewal in the continuity of the one subject Church which the Lord has given to us. She is a subject which increases in time and develops, yet always remains the same, the one subject of the journeying People of God.

The hermeneutic of discontinuity risks ending in a split between the pre-Conciliar Church and the post-Conciliar Church. It asserts that the texts of the Council as such do not yet express the true spirit of the Council. It claims that they are the result of compromises in which, to reach unanimity, it was found necessary to keep and reconfirm many old things that are now pointless. However, the true spirit of the Council is to be found not in these compromises but instead in the impulses toward the new that are contained in the texts.

These innovations alone were supposed to represent the true spirit of the Council, and starting from and in conformity with them, it would be possible to move ahead. Precisely because the texts would only imperfectly reflect the true spirit of the Council and its newness, it would be necessary to go courageously beyond the texts and make room for the newness in which the Council's deepest intention would be expressed, even if it were still vague.

In a word: it would be necessary to follow not the texts of the Council but its spirit. In this way, obviously, a vast margin was left open for the question on how this spirit should subsequently be defined and room was consequently made for every whim.

The nature of a Council as such is therefore basically misunderstood. In this way, it is considered as a sort of constituent that eliminates an old constitution and creates a new one. However, the Constituent Assembly needs a mandator and then confirmation by the mandator: in other words, the people the constitution must serve. The Fathers had no such mandate, and no one had ever given them one; nor could anyone have given them one because the essential constitution of the Church comes from the Lord and was given to us so that we might attain eternal life and, starting from this perspective, be able to illuminate life in time and time itself.

Through the Sacrament they have received, bishops are stewards of the Lord's gift. They are 'stewards of the mysteries of God' (1 Cor.

4.1); as such, they must be found to be 'faithful' and 'wise' (cf. Lk. 12.41–8). This requires them to administer the Lord's gift in the right way, so that it is not left concealed in some hiding place but bears fruit, and the Lord may end by saying to the administrator: 'Since you were dependable in a small matter I will put you in charge of larger affairs' (cf. Mt. 25.14–30; Lk. 19.11–27).

These Gospel parables express the dynamic of fidelity required in the Lord's service; and through them it becomes clear that, as in a Council, the dynamic and fidelity must converge.

The hermeneutic of discontinuity is countered by the hermeneutic of reform, as it was presented first by Pope John XXIII in his speech inaugurating the Council on 11 October 1962 and later by Pope Paul VI in his discourse for the conclusion of the Council, on 7 December 1965.

Here I shall cite only John XXIII's well-known words, which unequivocally express this hermeneutic when he says that the Council wishes 'to transmit the doctrine, pure and integral, without any attenuation or distortion'. And he continues: 'Our duty is not only to guard this precious treasure, as if we were concerned only with antiquity, but to dedicate ourselves with an earnest will and without fear to that work which our era demands of us.'

It is necessary that 'adherence to all the teaching of the Church in its entirety and preciseness' be presented in 'faithful and perfect conformity to the authentic doctrine, which, however, should be studied and expounded through the methods of research and through the literary forms of modern thought. The substance of the ancient doctrine of the deposit of faith is one thing, and the way in which it is presented is another', retaining the same meaning and message.[3]

It is clear that this commitment to expressing a specific truth in a new way demands new thinking on this truth and a new and vital relationship with it; it is also clear that new words can only develop if they come from an informed understanding of the truth expressed and, on the other hand, that a reflection on faith also requires that this faith be lived. In this regard, the programme that Pope John XXIII proposed was extremely demanding; indeed, just as the synthesis of fidelity and dynamic is demanding.

However, wherever this interpretation guided the implementation of the Council, new life developed and new fruit ripened. Forty years after the Council, we can show that the positive is far greater and livelier than it appeared to be in the turbulent years around 1968. Today we see that, although the good seed developed slowly, it is nonetheless growing; and our deep gratitude for the work done by the Council is likewise growing.

In his Discourse closing the Council, Paul VI pointed out a further specific reason why a hermeneutic of discontinuity can seem convincing.

In the great dispute about man which marks the modern epoch, the Council had to focus, in particular, on the theme of anthropology. It had to question the relationship between the Church and her faith on the one hand, and between man and the contemporary world on the other.[4] The question becomes even clearer if, instead of the generic term 'contemporary world', we opt for another one that is more precise: the Council had to determine in a new way the relationship between the Church and the modern era.

This relationship had a somewhat stormy beginning with the case of Galileo. It was then totally interrupted when Kant described 'religion within pure reason' and when, in the radical phase of the French Revolution, an image of the state and the human being was disseminated that scarcely longer wanted to allow the Church any room at all.

In the nineteenth century, under Pius IX, the clash between the Church's faith and a radical liberalism and the natural sciences – which also claimed to embrace with their knowledge the whole of reality to its limit, stubbornly proposing to make the 'hypothesis of God' superfluous – had elicited from the Church a bitter and radical condemnation of this spirit of the modern age. Thus, it seemed that there was no longer any milieu open to a positive and fruitful understanding, and the rejection by those who felt they were the representatives of the modern era was also drastic.

In the meantime, however, the modern age had also experienced developments. People came to realize that the American Revolution was offering a model of a modern State that differed from the theoretical model, with radical tendencies, that had emerged during the second phase of the French Revolution.

The natural sciences were beginning to reflect more and more clearly their own limitations imposed by their own method, which, despite achieving great things, was nevertheless unable to grasp the global nature of reality.

So it was that both parties were gradually beginning to open up to each other. In the period between the two world wars and especially after the Second World War, Catholic statesmen demonstrated that a modern secular state could exist that was not neutral regarding values but alive, drawing from the great ethical sources opened by Christianity.

Catholic social doctrine, as it gradually developed, became an important model between radical liberalism and the Marxist theory of the state. The natural sciences, which without reservation professed a method of their own to which God was barred access, realized ever more clearly that this method did not include the whole of reality. Hence, they once again opened their doors to God, knowing that reality is greater than the naturalistic method and all that it can encompass.

It might be said that three circles of questions had formed which then, at the time of the Second Vatican Council, were expecting an answer. First of all, the relationship between faith and modern science had to be redefined. Furthermore, this concerned not only the natural sciences but also historical science for, in one particular school, the historical–critical method claimed to have the last word on the interpretation of the Bible and, demanding total exclusivity for its interpretation of Sacred Scripture, was opposed to important points in the interpretation elaborated by the faith of the Church.

Second, it was necessary to give a new definition to the relationship between the Church and the modern state that would make room impartially for citizens of various religions and ideologies, merely assuming responsibility for an orderly and tolerant coexistence among them and for the freedom to practise their own religion.

Third, linked more generally to this was the problem of religious tolerance – a question that required a new definition of the relationship between the Christian faith and the world religions. In particular, before the recent crimes of the Nazi regime and, in general, with a retrospective look at a long and difficult history, it was necessary to evaluate and define in a new way the relationship between the Church and the faith of Israel.

These are all subjects of great importance: they were the great themes of the second part of the Council, on which it is impossible to reflect more broadly in this context. It is clear that in all these sectors, which all together form a single problem, some kind of discontinuity might emerge. Indeed, a discontinuity had been revealed but one in which, after the various distinctions between concrete historical situations and their requirements had been made, the continuity of principles proved not to have been abandoned. It is easy to miss this fact at a first glance.

It is precisely in this combination of continuity and discontinuity at different levels that the very nature of true reform consists. In this process of innovation in continuity we must learn to understand more practically than before that the Church's decisions on contingent matters – for example, certain practical forms of liberalism or a free interpretation of the Bible – should necessarily be contingent themselves, precisely because they refer to a specific reality that is changeable in itself. It was necessary to learn to recognize that in these decisions it is only the principles that express the permanent aspect, since they remain as an undercurrent, motivating decisions from within.

On the other hand, not so permanent are the practical forms that depend on the historical situation and are therefore subject to change.

Basic decisions, therefore, continue to be well grounded, whereas the way they are applied to new contexts can change. Thus, for example, if religious freedom were to be considered an expression of the human inability to discover the truth and thus become a canonization of relativism, then this social and historical necessity is raised inappropriately to the metaphysical level and thus stripped of its true meaning. Consequently, it cannot be accepted by those who believe that the human person is capable of knowing the truth about God and, on the basis of the inner dignity of the truth, is bound to this knowledge.

It is quite different, on the other hand, to perceive religious freedom as a need that derives from human coexistence or, indeed, as an intrinsic consequence of the truth that cannot be externally imposed but that the person must adopt only through the process of conviction.

The Second Vatican Council, recognizing and making its own an essential principle of the modern state with the Decree on Religious Freedom, has recovered the deepest patrimony of the Church. By so doing she can be conscious of being in full harmony with the teaching of Jesus himself (cf. Mt. 22.21), as well as with the Church of the martyrs of all time. The ancient Church naturally prayed for the emperors and political leaders out of duty (cf. 1 Tim. 2.2); but while she prayed for the emperors, she refused to worship them and thereby clearly rejected the religion of the state.

The martyrs of the early Church died for their faith in that God who was revealed in Jesus Christ, and for this very reason they also died for freedom of conscience and the freedom to profess one's own faith – a profession that no State can impose but which, instead, can only be claimed with God's grace in freedom of conscience. A missionary Church known for proclaiming her message to all peoples must necessarily work for the freedom of the faith. She desires to transmit the gift of the truth that exists for one and all.

At the same time, she assures peoples and their governments that she does not wish to destroy their identity and culture by doing so, but wishes to give them, on the contrary, a response which, in their innermost depths, they are waiting for – a response with which the multiplicity of cultures is not lost but instead unity between men and women increases and thus also peace between peoples.

The Second Vatican Council, with its new definition of the relationship between the faith of the Church and certain essential elements of modern thought, has reviewed or even corrected certain historical decisions, but in this apparent discontinuity it has actually preserved and deepened her innermost nature and true identity.

The Church, both before and after the Council, was and is the same Church, one, holy, Catholic and apostolic, journeying on through time; she continues 'her pilgrimage amid the persecutions of the world and the consolations of God', proclaiming the death of the Lord until he comes (cf. *Lumen Gentium,* n. 8).

Those who expected that with this fundamental 'yes' to the modern era all tensions would be dispelled and that the 'openness towards the world' accordingly achieved would transform everything into pure harmony, had underestimated the inner tensions as well as the contradictions inherent in the modern epoch.

They had underestimated the perilous frailty of human nature, which has been a threat to human progress in every period of history and in every historical constellation. These dangers, with the new possibilities and new power of man over matter and over himself, did not disappear but instead acquired new dimensions: a look at the history of the present day shows this clearly.

In our time too the Church remains a 'sign that will be opposed' (Lk. 2.34): not without reason did Pope John Paul II, then still a Cardinal, give this title to the theme for the Spiritual Exercises he preached in 1976 to Pope Paul VI and the Roman Curia. The Council could not have intended to abolish the Gospel's opposition to human dangers and errors.

On the contrary, it was certainly the Council's intention to overcome erroneous or superfluous contradictions in order to present to our world the requirement of the Gospel in its full greatness and purity.

The steps the Council took towards the modern era, which had rather vaguely been presented as 'openness to the world', belong in short to the perennial problem of the relationship between faith and reason that is re-emerging in ever new forms. The situation that the Council had to face can certainly be compared to events in previous epochs.

In his First Letter St Peter urged Christians always to be ready to give an answer (*apo-logia*) to anyone who asked them for the *logos*, the reason for their faith (cf. 1 Pet. 3.15).

This meant that biblical faith had to be discussed and come into contact with Greek culture and learn to recognize through interpretation the separating line but also the convergence and the affinity between them in the one reason, given by God.

When, in the thirteenth century, through the Jewish and Arab philosophers, Aristotelian thought came into contact with medieval Christianity formed in the Platonic tradition and faith and reason risked entering an irreconcilable contradiction, it was above all St Thomas Aquinas who mediated the new encounter between faith and Aristotelian philosophy, thereby setting faith in a positive relationship with the form of reason prevalent in his time. There is no doubt that the wearing dispute between modern reason and the Christian faith, which had begun negatively with the Galileo case, went through many phases, but with the Second Vatican Council the time came when broad new thinking was required.

Its content was certainly only roughly traced in the conciliar texts, but this determined its essential direction, so that the dialogue between reason and faith, particularly important today, found its bearings on the basis of the Second Vatican Council.

This dialogue must now be developed with great open-mindedness but also with that clear discernment that the world rightly expects of us in this very moment. Thus, today we can look with gratitude at the Second Vatican Council: if we interpret and implement it guided by a right hermeneutic, it can be and can become increasingly powerful for the ever-necessary renewal of the Church.

Lastly, should I perhaps recall once again that 19 April this year, on which, to my great surprise, the College of Cardinals elected me as the successor of Pope John Paul II, as a successor of St Peter on the chair of the bishop of Rome? Such an office was far beyond anything I could ever have imagined as my vocation. It was, therefore, only with a great act of trust in God that I was able to say in obedience my 'Yes' to this choice. Now, as then, I also ask you all for your prayer, on whose power and support I rely.

At the same time, I would like to warmly thank all those who have welcomed me and still welcome me with great trust, goodness and understanding, accompanying me day after day with their prayers.

Christmas is now at hand. The Lord God did not counter the threats of history with external power, as we human beings would expect according to the prospects of our world. His weapon is goodness. He revealed himself as a child, born in a stable. This is precisely how he counters with his power, completely different from the destructive powers of violence. In this very way he saves us. In this very way he shows us what saves.

In these days of Christmas, let us go to meet him full of trust, like the shepherds, like the Wise Men of the East. Let us ask Mary to lead us to the Lord. Let us ask him himself to make his face shine upon us. Let us ask him also to defeat the violence in the world and to make us experience the power of his goodness. With these sentiments, I warmly impart to you all my Apostolic Blessing.

3

Only With God Can We Create a Real Revolution

Apostolic Journey to Cologne on the
Occasion of the XX World Youth Day
Youth Vigil

ADDRESS OF HIS HOLINESS POPE
BENEDICT XVI
MARIENFELD, COLOGNE
SATURDAY, 20 AUGUST 2005

Dear young friends, in our pilgrimage with the mysterious Magi from the East, we have arrived at the moment which St Matthew describes in his Gospel with these words: 'Going into the house (over which the star had halted), they saw the child with Mary his mother, and they fell down and worshipped him' (Mt. 2.11). Outwardly, their journey was now over. They had reached their goal.

But at this point a new journey began for them, an inner pilgrimage which changed their whole lives. Their mental picture of the infant King they were expecting to find must have been very different. They had stopped at Jerusalem specifically in order to ask the King who lived there for news of the promised King who had been born. They knew that the world was in disorder, and for that reason their hearts were troubled.

They were sure that God existed and that he was a just and gentle God. And perhaps they also knew of the great prophecies of Israel foretelling a King who would be intimately united with God, a King who would restore order to the world, acting for God and in his name.

It was in order to seek this King that they had set off on their journey: deep within themselves they felt prompted to go in search of the true justice that can only come from God, and they wanted to serve this King, to fall prostrate at his feet and so play their part in the renewal of the world. They were among those 'who hunger and thirst for justice' (Mt. 5.6). This hunger and thirst had spurred them on in their pilgrimage; they had become pilgrims in search of the justice that they expected from God, intending to devote themselves to its service.

Even if those who had stayed at home may have considered them utopian dreamers, they were actually people with their feet on the ground, and they knew that in order to change the world it is necessary to have power. Hence they were hardly likely to seek the promised child anywhere but in the king's palace. Yet now they were bowing down before the child of poor people, and they soon came to realize that Herod, the king they had consulted, intended to use his power to lay a trap for him, forcing the family to flee into exile.

The new king, to whom they now paid homage, was quite unlike what they were expecting. In this way they had to learn that God is not as we usually imagine him to be. This was where their inner journey began. It started at the very moment when they knelt down before this child and recognized him as the promised king. But they still had to assimilate these joyful gestures internally.

They had to change their ideas about power, about God and about man, and in so doing, they also had to change themselves. Now they were able to see that God's power is not like that of the powerful of this world. God's ways are not as we imagine them or as we might wish them to be.

God does not enter into competition with earthly powers in this world. He does not marshal his divisions alongside other divisions. God did not send 12 legions of angels to assist Jesus in the Garden of Olives (cf. Mt. 26.53). He contrasts the noisy and ostentatious power of this world with the defenceless power of love, which succumbs to death on the Cross and dies ever anew throughout history; yet it is this same love which constitutes the new divine intervention that opposes injustice and ushers in the Kingdom of God.

God is different – this is what they now come to realize. And it means that they themselves must now become different; they must learn God's ways.

They had come to place themselves at the service of this king, to model their own kingship on his. That was the meaning of their act of homage, their adoration. Included in this were their gifts – gold, frankincense and myrrh – gifts offered to a king held to be divine. Adoration has a content, and it involves giving. Through this act of adoration, these men from the East wished to recognize the child as their king and to place their own power and potential at his disposal, and in this they were certainly on the right path.

By serving and following him, they wanted, together with him, to serve the cause of good and the cause of justice in the world. In this they were right.

Now, though, they have to learn that this cannot be achieved simply through issuing commands from a throne on high. Now they have to learn to give themselves: no lesser gift would be sufficient for this king. Now they have to learn that their lives must be conformed to this divine way of exercising power, to God's own way of being.

They must become men of truth, of justice, of goodness, of forgiveness, of mercy. They will no longer ask: how can this serve me? Instead, they will have to ask: how can I serve God's presence in the world? They must learn to lose their life and in this way to find it. Having left Jerusalem behind, they must not deviate from the path marked out by the true king, as they follow Jesus.

Dear friends, what does all this mean for us?

What we have just been saying about the nature of God being different, and about the way our lives must be shaped accordingly, sounds very fine, but remains rather vague and unfocused. That is why God has given us examples. The Magi from the East are just the first in a long procession of men and women who have constantly tried to gaze on God's star in their lives, going in search of the God who has drawn close to us and shows us the way.

It is the great multitude of the saints, both known and unknown, in whose lives the Lord has opened up the Gospel before us and turned over the pages; he has done this throughout history and he still does so today. In their lives, as if in a great picturebook, the riches of the Gospel are revealed. They are the shining path which God himself has traced throughout history and is still tracing today.

My venerable predecessor Pope John Paul II, who is with us at this moment, beatified and canonized a great many people from both the distant and the recent past. Through these individuals he wanted to show us how to be Christian, how to live life as it should be lived: according to God's way. The saints and the blessed did not doggedly seek their own happiness, but simply wanted to give themselves, because the light of Christ had shone upon them.

They show us the way to attain happiness; they show us how to be truly human. Through all the ups and downs of history, they were the true reformers who constantly rescued it from plunging into the valley of darkness; it was they who constantly shed upon it the light that was needed to make sense – even in the midst of suffering – of God's words spoken at the end of the work of creation: 'It is very good.'

One need only think of such figures as St Benedict, St Francis of Assisi, St Teresa of Ávila,

St Ignatius of Loyola, St Charles Borromeo, the founders of nineteenth-century religious orders who inspired and guided the social movement, or the saints of our own day: Maximilian Kolbe, Edith Stein, Mother Teresa, Padre Pio. In contemplating these figures we learn what it means 'to adore' and what it means to live according to the measure of the Child of Bethlehem, by the measure of Jesus Christ and of God himself.

The saints, as we said, are the true reformers. Now I want to express this in an even more radical way: only from the saints, only from God does true revolution come, the definitive way to change the world.

In the last century we experienced revolutions with a common programme: expecting nothing more from God, they assumed total responsibility for the cause of the world in order to change it. And this, as we saw, meant that a human and partial point of view was always taken as an absolute guiding principle. Absolutizing what is not absolute but relative is called totalitarianism. It does not liberate man, but takes away his dignity and enslaves him.

It is not ideologies that save the world, but only a return to the living God, our Creator, the guarantor of our freedom, the guarantor of what is really good and true. True revolution consists in simply turning to God, who is the measure of what is right and who at the same time is everlasting love. And what could ever save us apart from love?

Dear friends! Allow me to add just two brief thoughts.

There are many who speak of God; some even preach hatred and perpetrate violence in God's name. So it is important to discover the true face of God. The Magi from the East found it when they knelt down before the Child of Bethlehem. 'Anyone who has seen me has seen the Father,' said Jesus to Philip (Jn 14.9). In Jesus Christ, who allowed his heart to be pierced for us, the true face of God is seen. We will follow him together with the great multitude of those who went before us. Then we will be travelling along the right path.

This means that we are not constructing a private God, we are not constructing a private Jesus, but that we believe and worship the Jesus who is manifested to us by the sacred scriptures and who reveals himself to be alive in the great procession of the faithful called the Church, always alongside us and always before us.

There is much that could be criticized in the Church. We know this, and the Lord himself told us so: it is a net with good fish and bad fish, a field with wheat and darnel.

Pope John Paul II, as well as revealing the true face of the Church in the many saints that he canonized, also asked pardon for the wrong that was done in the course of history through the words and deeds of members of the Church. In this way he showed us our own true image and urged us to take our place, with all our faults and weaknesses, in the procession of the saints that began with the Magi from the East.

It is actually consoling to realize that there is darnel in the Church. In this way, despite all our defects, we can still hope to be counted among the disciples of Jesus, who came to call sinners.

The Church is like a human family, but at the same time it is also the great family of God, through which he establishes an overarching communion and unity that embraces every continent, culture and nation. So we are glad to belong to this great family that we see here; we are glad to have brothers and friends all over the world.

Here in Cologne we discover the joy of belonging to a family as vast as the world, including Heaven and earth, the past, the present, the future and every part of the earth. In this great band of pilgrims we walk side by side with Christ; we walk with the star that enlightens our history.

'Going into the house, they saw the child with Mary his mother, and they fell down and worshipped him' (Mt. 2.11). Dear friends, this is not a distant story that took place long ago. It is with us now. Here in the Sacred Host he is present before us and in our midst. As at that time, so now he is mysteriously veiled in a sacred silence; as at that time, it is here that the true face of God is revealed. For us he became a grain of wheat that falls on the ground and dies and bears fruit until the end of the world (cf. Jn 12.24).

He is present now as he was then in Bethlehem. He invites us to that inner pilgrimage which is called adoration. Let us set off on this pilgrimage of the spirit and let us ask him to be our guide.

Amen.

4

The Holocaust: A Warning Against Evil

Pastoral Visit of His Holiness Pope Benedict XVI in Poland

ADDRESS BY THE HOLY FATHER
VISIT TO THE AUSCHWITZ CAMP
AUSCHWITZ-BIRKENAU, 28 MAY 2006

To speak in this place of horror, in this place where unprecedented mass crimes were committed against God and man, is almost impossible – and it is particularly difficult and troubling for a Christian, for a Pope from Germany. In a place like this, words fail; in the end, there can only be a dread silence – a silence which is itself a heartfelt cry to God: why, Lord, did you remain silent?

How could you tolerate all this? In silence, then, we bow our heads before the endless line of those who suffered and were put to death here; yet our silence becomes in turn a plea for forgiveness and reconciliation, a plea to the living God never to let this happen again.

Twenty-seven years ago, on 7 June 1979, Pope John Paul II stood in this place. He said: 'I come here today as a pilgrim. As you know, I have been here many times. So many times! And many times I have gone down to Maximilian Kolbe's death cell, paused before the wall of death, and walked amid the ruins of the Birkenau ovens. It was impossible for me not to come here as Pope.' Pope John Paul came here as a son of that people which, along with the Jewish people, suffered most in this place and, in general, throughout the war. 'Six million Poles lost their lives during the Second World War: a fifth of the nation,' he reminded us. Here too he solemnly called for respect for human rights and the rights of nations, as his predecessors John XXIII and Paul VI had done before him, and added: 'The one who speaks these words is ... the son of a nation which in its history has suffered greatly from others. He says this, not to accuse, but to remember. He speaks in the name of all those nations whose rights are being violated and disregarded.'

Pope John Paul II came here as a son of the Polish people. I come here today as a son of the German people. For this very reason I can and must echo his words: I could not fail to come here. I had to come. It is a duty before the truth and the just due of all who suffered here, a duty before God, for me to come here as the successor of Pope John Paul II and as a son of the German people – a son of that people over which a ring of criminals rose to power by false promises of future greatness and the recovery of the nation's honour, prominence and prosperity, but also through terror and intimidation, with the result that our people was used and abused as an instrument of their thirst for destruction and power. Yes, I could not fail to come here. On 7 June 1979 I came as the archbishop of Munich–Freising, along with many other bishops who accompanied the Pope, listened to his words and joined in his prayer. In 1980 I came back to this dreadful place with a delegation of German bishops, appalled by its evil, yet grateful for the fact that above its dark clouds the star of reconciliation had emerged. This is the same reason why I have come here today: to implore the grace of reconciliation – first of all from God, who alone can open and purify our hearts, from the men and women who suffered here, and finally the grace of reconciliation for all those who, at this hour of our history, are suffering in new ways from the power of hatred and the violence which hatred spawns.

How many questions arise in this place! Constantly the question comes up: where was God in those days? Why was he silent? How could he permit this endless slaughter, this triumph of evil? The words of Psalm 44 come to mind, Israel's lament for its woes: 'You have broken us in the haunt of jackals, and covered us with deep darkness ... because of you we are being killed all day long, and accounted as sheep for the slaughter. Rouse yourself! Why do you sleep, O Lord? Awake, do not cast us off forever! Why do you hide your face? Why do you forget our affliction and oppression? For we sink down to the dust; our bodies cling to the ground. Rise up, come to our help! Redeem us for the sake of your steadfast love!' (Ps. 44.19, 22–6). This cry of anguish, which Israel raised to God in its suffering, at moments of deep distress, is also the cry for help raised by all those who in every age – yesterday, today and tomorrow – suffer for the love of God, for the love of truth and goodness. How many they are, even in our own day!

We cannot peer into God's mysterious plan – we see only piecemeal, and we would be wrong to set ourselves up as judges of God and history.

Then we would not be defending man, but only contributing to his downfall. No – when all is said and done, we must continue to cry out humbly yet insistently to God: rouse yourself! Do not forget mankind, your creature! And our cry to God must also be a cry that pierces our very heart, a cry that awakens within us God's hidden presence – so that his power, the power he has planted in our hearts, will not be buried or choked within us by the mire of selfishness, pusillanimity, indifference or opportunism.

Let us cry out to God, with all our hearts, at the present hour, when new misfortunes befall us, when all the forces of darkness seem to issue anew from human hearts: whether it is the abuse of God's name as a means of justifying senseless violence against innocent persons, or the cynicism which refuses to acknowledge God and ridicules faith in him. Let us cry out to God, that he may draw men and women to conversion and help them to see that violence does not bring peace but only generates more violence – a morass of devastation in which everyone is ultimately the loser. The God in whom we believe is a God of reason – a reason, to be sure, which is not a kind of cold mathematics of the universe, but is one with love and with goodness. We make our prayer to God and we appeal to humanity, that this reason, the logic of love and the recognition of the power of reconciliation and peace, may prevail over the threats arising from irrationalism or from a spurious and godless reason.

The place where we are standing is a place of memory, it is the place of the Shoah. The past is never simply the past. It always has something to say to us; it tells us the paths to take and the paths not to take. Like John Paul II, I have walked alongside the inscriptions in various languages erected in memory of those who died here: inscriptions in Belarusian, Czech, German, French, Greek, Hebrew, Croatian, Italian, Yiddish, Hungarian, Dutch, Norwegian, Polish, Russian, Romani, Romanian, Slovak, Serbian, Ukrainian, Judaeo-Spanish and English. All these inscriptions speak of human grief; they give us a glimpse of the cynicism of that regime which treated men and women as material objects, and failed to see them as persons embodying the image of God. Some inscriptions are pointed reminders. There is one in Hebrew. The rulers of the Third Reich wanted to crush the entire Jewish people, to cancel it from the register of the peoples of the earth. Thus the words of the Psalm, 'We are being killed, accounted as sheep for the slaughter', were fulfilled in a terrifying way. Deep down, those vicious criminals, by wiping out this people, wanted to kill the God who called Abraham, who spoke on Sinai and laid down principles to serve as a guide for mankind, principles that are eternally valid. If this people, by its very existence, was a witness to the God who spoke to humanity and took us to himself, then that God finally had to die and power had to belong to man alone – to those men, who thought that by force they had made themselves masters of the world. By destroying Israel, by the Shoah, they ultimately wanted to tear up the taproot of the Christian faith and to replace it with a faith of their own invention: faith in the rule of man, the rule of the powerful.

Then there is the inscription in Polish. First and foremost they wanted to eliminate the cultural elite, thus erasing the Polish people as an autonomous historical subject and reducing it, to the extent that it continued to exist, to slavery. Another inscription offering a pointed reminder is the one written in the language of the Sinti and Roma people. Here too the plan was to wipe out a whole people which lives by migrating among other peoples. They were seen as part of the refuse of world history, in an ideology which valued only the empirically useful; everything else, according to this view, was to be written off as *lebensunwertes Leben* – life unworthy of being lived. There is also the inscription in Russian, which commemorates the tremendous loss of life endured by the Russian soldiers who combated the Nazi reign of terror; but this inscription also reminds us that their mission had a tragic twofold effect: it set the peoples free from one dictatorship, but the same peoples were thereby subjected to a new one, that of Stalin and the Communist system.

The other inscriptions, written in Europe's many languages, also speak to us of the sufferings of men and women from the whole continent. They would stir our hearts profoundly if we remembered the victims not merely in general, but rather saw the faces of the individual persons who ended up here in this abyss of terror. I felt a deep urge to pause in a particular way before the inscription in German. It evokes the face of Edith Stein, Teresia Benedicta a Cruce: a woman, Jewish and German, who disappeared along with her sister into the black night of the Nazi concentration camp; as a Christian and a Jew, she accepted death with her people and for them. The Germans who had been brought to Auschwitz-Birkenau and met their death here were considered as *Abschaum der Nation* – the refuse of the nation. Today we gratefully hail them as witnesses to the truth and goodness which even among our people were not eclipsed.

We are grateful to them, because they did not submit to the power of evil, and now they stand before us like lights shining in a dark night. With profound respect and gratitude, then, let us bow our heads before all those who, like the three young men in Babylon facing death in the fiery furnace, could respond: 'Only our God can deliver us. But even if he does not, be it known to you, O King, that we will not serve your gods and we will not worship the golden statue that you have set up' (cf. Dan. 3.17ff.).

Yes, behind these inscriptions is hidden the fate of countless human beings. They jar our memory, they touch our hearts. They have no desire to instil hatred in us: instead, they show us the terrifying effect of hatred. Their desire is to help our reason to see evil as evil and to reject it; their desire is to enkindle in us the courage to do good and to resist evil. They want to make us feel the sentiments expressed in the words that Sophocles placed on the lips of Antigone, as she contemplated the horror all around her: my nature is not to join in hate but to join in love.

By God's grace, together with the purification of memory demanded by this place of horror, a number of initiatives have sprung up with the aim of imposing a limit upon evil and confirming goodness. Just now I was able to bless the Centre for Dialogue and Prayer. In the immediate neighbourhood the Carmelite nuns carry on their life of hiddenness, knowing that they are united in a special way to the mystery of Christ's Cross and reminding us of the faith of Christians, which declares that God himself descended into the hell of suffering and suffers with us. In Oświęcim is the Centre of St Maximilian Kolbe, and the International Centre for Education about Auschwitz and the Holocaust. There is also the International House for Meetings of Young people. Near one of the old prayer houses is the Jewish Centre. Finally the Academy for Human Rights is presently being established. So there is hope that this place of horror will gradually become a place for constructive thinking, and that remembrance will foster resistance to evil and the triumph of love.

At Auschwitz-Birkenau humanity walked through a 'valley of darkness'. And so, here in this place, I would like to end with a prayer of trust – with one of the Psalms of Israel which is also a prayer of Christians:

The Lord is my shepherd, I shall not want. He makes me lie down in green pastures; he leads me beside still waters; he restores my soul. He leads me in right paths for his name's sake. Even though I walk through the valley of the shadow of death, I fear no evil; for you are with me; your rod and your staff – they comfort me ... I shall dwell in the house of the Lord my whole life long. (Ps. 23.1–4, 6).

Reason: A Guard Against Pure Subjectivism

*Apostolic Journey of his Holiness Benedict XVI
to Munich, Altötting and Regensburg (9–14
September 2006)
Meeting with the Representatives of Science*

LECTURE OF THE HOLY FATHER
AULA MAGNA OF THE UNIVERSITY OF
REGENSBURG TUESDAY, 12 SEPTEMBER
2006

Your Eminences, Your Magnificences, Your
Excellencies,
Distinguished Ladies and Gentlemen,

It is a moving experience for me to be back again in the university and to be able once again to give a lecture at this podium. I think back to those years when, after a pleasant period at the Freisinger Hochschule, I began teaching at the University of Bonn. That was in 1959, in the days of the old university made up of ordinary professors. The various chairs had neither assistants nor secretaries, but in recompense there was much direct contact with students and, in particular, among the professors themselves. We would meet before and after lessons in the rooms of the teaching staff. There was a lively exchange with historians, philosophers, philologists and, naturally, between the two theological faculties.

Once a semester there was a *dies academicus*, when professors from every faculty appeared before the students of the entire university, making possible a genuine experience of *universitas* – something that you too, Magnificent Rector, just mentioned – the experience, in other words, of the fact that despite our specializations which at times make it difficult to communicate with each other, we made up a whole, working in everything on the basis of a single rationality with its various aspects and sharing responsibility for the right use of reason – this reality became a lived experience. The university was also very proud of its two theological faculties. It was clear that, by inquiring about the reasonableness of faith, they too carried out a work which is necessarily part of the 'whole' of the *universitas scientiarum*, even if not everyone could share the faith which theologians seek to correlate with reason as a whole. This profound sense of coherence within the universe of reason was not troubled, even when it was once reported that a colleague had said there was something odd about our university: it had two faculties devoted to something that did not exist – God. That even in the face of such radical scepticism it is still necessary and reasonable to raise the question of God through the use of reason, and to do so in the context of the tradition of the Christian faith: this, within the university as a whole, was accepted without question.

I was reminded of all this recently, when I read the edition by Professor Theodore Khoury (Münster) of part of the dialogue carried on – perhaps in 1391 in the winter barracks near Ankara – by the erudite Byzantine emperor Manuel II Palaeologus and an educated Persian on the subject of Christianity and Islam, and the truth of both.[1] It was presumably the emperor himself who set down this dialogue, during the siege of Constantinople between 1394 and 1402; and this would explain why his arguments are given in greater detail than those of his Persian interlocutor.[2] The dialogue ranges widely over the structures of faith contained in the Bible and in the Qur'an, and deals especially with the image of God and of man, while necessarily returning repeatedly to the relationship between – as they were called – three 'Laws' or 'rules of life': the Old Testament, the New Testament and the Qur'an. It is not my intention to discuss this question in the present lecture; here I would like to discuss only one point – itself rather marginal to the dialogue as a whole – which, in the context of the issue of 'faith and reason', I found interesting and which can serve as the starting point for my reflections on this issue.

In the seventh conversation (διάλεξις – controversy) edited by Professor Khoury, the emperor touches on the theme of the holy war. The emperor must have known that surah 2, verse 256, reads: 'There is no compulsion in religion.' According to some of the experts, this is probably one of the surahs of the early period, when Mohammed was still powerless and under threat. But naturally the emperor also knew the instructions, developed later and recorded in the Qur'an, concerning holy war. Without descending to details, such as the difference in treatment accorded to those who have the 'Book' and the 'infidels', he addresses his interlocutor with a startling brusqueness, a brusqueness that we find unacceptable, on the central question about the relationship between religion and violence in general, saying: 'Show me just what Mohammed brought that was new, and there you will find things only evil and inhuman, such as his command to spread by the sword the faith he preached.'[3] The emperor, after having expressed himself so forcefully, goes on to explain in detail the reasons why spreading the faith through violence is something unreasonable. Violence is incompatible with the nature of God and the nature of the soul. 'God,' he says,

> is not pleased by blood – and not acting reasonably (σὺν λόγω) is contrary to God's nature. Faith is born of the soul, not the body. Whoever would lead someone to faith needs the ability to speak well and to reason properly, without violence and threats ... To convince a reasonable soul, one does not need a strong arm, or weapons of any kind, or any other means of threatening a person with death.[4]

The decisive statement in this argument against violent conversion is this: not to act in accordance with reason is contrary to God's nature.[5] The editor, Theodore Khoury, observes: 'For the emperor, as a Byzantine shaped by Greek philosophy, this statement is self-evident. But for Muslim teaching, God is absolutely transcendent. His will is not bound up with any of our categories, even that of rationality.'[6] Here Khoury quotes a work of the noted French Islamist Roger Arnaldez, who points out that Ibn Hazm went so far as to state that God is not bound even by his own word, and that nothing would oblige him to reveal the truth to us. Were it God's will, we would even have to practise idolatry.[7]

At this point, as far as understanding of God and thus the concrete practice of religion is concerned, we are faced with an unavoidable dilemma. Is the conviction that acting unreasonably contradicts God's nature merely a Greek idea, or is it always and intrinsically true? I believe that here we can see the profound harmony between what is Greek in the best sense of the word and the biblical understanding of faith in God. Modifying the first verse of the Book of Genesis, the first verse of the whole Bible, John began the prologue of his Gospel with the words: 'In the beginning was the λόγος.' This is the very word used by the emperor: God acts, σὺν λόγω, with *logos*. *Logos* means both reason and word – a reason that is creative and capable of self-communication, precisely as reason. John thus spoke the final word on the biblical concept of God, and in this word all the often toilsome and tortuous threads of biblical faith find their culmination and synthesis. In the beginning was the *logos*, and the *logos* is God, says the evangelist. The encounter between the biblical message and Greek thought did not happen by chance. The vision of St Paul, who saw the roads to Asia barred and in a dream saw a Macedonian man plead with him, 'Come over to Macedonia and help us!' (cf. Acts 16.6–10) – this vision can be interpreted as a 'distillation' of the intrinsic necessity of a rapprochement between biblical faith and Greek inquiry.

In point of fact, this rapprochement had been going on for some time. The mysterious name of God, revealed from the burning bush, a name that separates this God from all other divinities with their many names and simply asserts being, 'I am', already presents a challenge to the notion of myth, to which Socrates' attempt to vanquish and transcend myth stands in close analogy.[8] Within the Old Testament, the process which started at the burning bush came to new maturity at the time of the exile, when the God of Israel, an Israel now deprived of its land and worship, was proclaimed as the God of heaven and earth and described in a simple formula which echoes the words uttered at the burning bush: 'I am'. This new understanding of God is accompanied by a kind of enlightenment, which finds stark expression in the mockery of gods who are merely the work of human hands (cf. Ps. 115). Thus, despite the bitter conflict with those Hellenistic rulers who sought to accommodate it forcibly to the customs and idolatrous cult of the Greeks, biblical faith, in the Hellenistic period, encountered the best of Greek thought at a deep level, resulting in a mutual enrichment evident especially in the later wisdom literature. Today we know that the Greek translation of the Old Testament produced at Alexandria – the Septuagint – is more than a simple (and in that sense really less than satisfactory) translation of the Hebrew text: it is an independent textual witness and a distinct and important step in the history of revelation, one that brought about this encounter in a way that was decisive for the birth and spread of Christianity.[9] A profound encounter of faith and reason is taking place here, an encounter between genuine enlightenment and religion. From the very heart of Christian faith and, at the same time, the heart of Greek thought now joined to faith, Manuel II was able to say: not to act 'with *logos*' is contrary to God's nature.

In all honesty, one must observe that in the late Middle Ages we find trends in theology which would sunder this synthesis between the Greek spirit and the Christian spirit. In contrast with the so-called intellectualism of Augustine and Thomas, there arose with Duns Scotus a voluntarism which, in its later developments, led to the claim that we can only know God's *voluntas ordinata*. Beyond this is the realm of God's freedom, in virtue of which he could have done the opposite of everything he has actually done. This gives rise to positions that clearly approach that of Ibn Hazm and might even lead to the image of a capricious God, who is not even bound to truth and goodness. God's transcendence and otherness are so exalted that our reason, our sense of the true and good, are no longer an authentic mirror of God, whose deepest possibilities remain eternally unattainable and hidden behind his actual decisions. As opposed to this, the faith of the Church has always insisted that between God and us, between his eternal creator spirit and our created reason there exists a real analogy, in which – as the Fourth Lateran Council stated in 1215 – unlikeness remains infinitely greater than likeness, yet not to the point of abolishing analogy and its language. God does not become more divine when we push him away from us in a sheer, impenetrable voluntarism; rather, the truly divine God is the God who has revealed himself as *logos* and, as *logos*, has acted and continues to act lovingly on our behalf. Certainly, love, as St Paul says, 'transcends' knowledge and is thereby capable of perceiving more than thought alone (cf. Eph. 3.19); nonetheless it continues to be love of the God who is *Logos*. Consequently, Christian worship is, again to quote Paul – 'λογικὴ λατρεία', worship in harmony with the eternal Word and with our reason (cf. Rom. 12.1).[10]

This inner rapprochement between biblical faith and Greek philosophical inquiry was an event of decisive importance not only from the standpoint of the history of religions but also from that of world history – it is an event that concerns us even today. Given this convergence, it is not surprising that Christianity, despite its origins and some significant developments in the East, finally took on its historically decisive character in Europe. We can also express this the other way round: this convergence, with the subsequent addition of the Roman heritage, created Europe and remains the foundation of what can rightly be called Europe.

The thesis that the critically purified Greek heritage forms an integral part of Christian faith has been countered by the call for a de-Hellenization of Christianity – a call which has more and more dominated theological discussions since the beginning of the modern age. Viewed more closely, three stages can be observed in the programme of de-Hellenization. Although interconnected, they are clearly distinct from one another in their motivations and objectives.[11]

De-Hellenization first emerges in connection with the postulates of the Reformation in the sixteenth century. Looking at the tradition of scholastic theology, the Reformers thought they were confronted with a faith system totally conditioned by philosophy – that is to say, an articulation of the faith based on an alien system of thought. As a result, faith appeared no longer as a living historical Word but as one element of an overarching philosophical system. The principle of *sola scriptura*, on the other hand, sought faith in its pure, primordial form, as originally found in the biblical Word. Metaphysics appeared as a premise derived from another source, from which faith had to be liberated in order to become once more fully itself. When Kant stated that he needed to set thinking aside in order to make room for faith, he carried this programme forward with a radicalism that the Reformers could never have foreseen. He thus anchored faith exclusively in practical reason, denying it access to reality as a whole.

The liberal theology of the nineteenth and twentieth centuries ushered in a second stage in the process of de-Hellenization, with Adolf von Harnack as its outstanding representative. When I was a student, and in the early years of my teaching, this programme was highly influential in Catholic theology too. It took as its point of departure Pascal's distinction between the God of the philosophers and the God of Abraham, Isaac and Jacob. In my inaugural lecture at Bonn in 1959, I tried to address the issue,[12] and I do not intend to repeat here what I said on that occasion, but I would like to describe at least briefly what was new about this second stage of de-Hellenization. Harnack's central idea was to return simply to the man Jesus and to his simple message, underneath the accretions of theology and indeed of Hellenization: this simple message was seen as the culmination of the religious development of humanity. Jesus was said to have put an end to worship in favour of morality. In the end he was presented as the father of a humanitarian moral message. Fundamentally, Harnack's goal was to bring Christianity back into harmony with modern reason, liberating it, that is to say, from seemingly philosophical and theological elements, such as faith in Christ's divinity and the triune God. In this sense, historical–critical exegesis of the New Testament, as he saw it, restored to theology its place within the university: theology, for Harnack, is something essentially historical and therefore strictly scientific. What it is able to say critically about Jesus is, so to speak, an expression of practical reason, and consequently it can take its rightful place within the university.

Behind this thinking lies the modern self-limitation of reason, classically expressed in Kant's 'Critiques', but in the meantime further radicalized by the impact of the natural sciences. This modern concept of reason is based, to put it briefly, on a synthesis between Platonism (Cartesianism) and empiricism, a synthesis confirmed by the success of technology. On the one hand it presupposes the mathematical structure of matter, its intrinsic rationality, which makes it possible to understand how matter works and use it efficiently: this basic premise is, so to speak, the Platonic element in the modern understanding of nature. On the other hand there is nature's capacity to be exploited for our purposes, and here only the possibility of verification or falsification through experimentation can yield decisive certainty. The weight between the two poles can, depending on the circumstances, shift from one side to the other. As strongly positivistic a thinker as Jacques Monod has declared himself a convinced Platonist/Cartesian.

This gives rise to two principles that are crucial for the issue we have raised. First, only the kind of certainty resulting from the interplay of mathematical and empirical elements can be considered scientific. Anything that would claim to be science must be measured against this criterion. Hence the human sciences, such as history, psychology, sociology and philosophy, attempt to conform themselves to this canon of scientificity. A second point, which is important for our reflections, is that by its very nature this method excludes the question of God, making it appear an unscientific or pre-scientific question. Consequently, we are faced with a reduction of the radius of science and reason, one that needs to be questioned.

I will return to this problem later. In the meantime, it must be observed that from this standpoint any attempt to maintain theology's claim to be 'scientific' would end up reducing Christianity to a mere fragment of its former self. But we must say more: if science as a whole is this and this alone, then it is man himself who ends up being reduced, for the specifically human questions about our origin and destiny, the questions raised by religion and ethics, then have no place within the purview of collective reason as defined by 'science', so understood, and must thus be relegated to the realm of the subjective. The subject then decides, on the basis of his or her experiences, what he or she considers tenable in matters of religion, and the subjective 'conscience' becomes the sole arbiter of what is ethical. In this way, though, ethics and religion lose their power to create a community and become a completely personal matter. This is a dangerous state of affairs for humanity, as we see from the disturbing pathologies of religion and reason that necessarily erupt when reason is so reduced that questions of religion and ethics no longer concern it. Attempts to construct an ethic from the rules of evolution, or from psychology and sociology, end up being simply inadequate.

Before I draw the conclusions to which all this has been leading, I must briefly refer to the third stage of de-Hellenization, which is now in progress. In the light of our experience with cultural pluralism, it is often said nowadays that the synthesis with Hellenism achieved in the early Church was an initial inculturation which ought not to be binding on other cultures. The latter are said to have the right to return to the simple message of the New Testament prior to that inculturation, in order to inculturate it anew in their own particular milieux. This thesis is not simply false but is coarse and lacking in precision. The New Testament was written in Greek and bears the imprint of the Greek spirit, which had already come to maturity as the Old Testament developed. True, there are elements in the evolution of the early Church which do not have to be integrated into all cultures. Nonetheless, the fundamental decisions made about the relationship between faith and the use of human reason are part of the faith itself; they are developments consonant with the nature of faith itself.

And so I come to my conclusion. This attempt, painted with broad strokes, at a critique of modern reason from within has nothing to do with putting the clock back to the time before the Enlightenment and rejecting the insights of the modern age. The positive aspects of modernity are to be acknowledged unreservedly: we are all grateful for the marvellous possibilities that it has opened up for mankind and for the progress in humanity that has been granted to us. The scientific ethos, moreover, is – as you yourself mentioned, magnificent rector – the will to be obedient to the truth, and, as such, it embodies an attitude that belongs to the essential decisions of the Christian spirit. The intention here is one not of retrenchment or negative criticism, but of broadening our concept of reason and its application. While we rejoice in the new possibilities open to humanity, we also see the dangers arising from these possibilities and we must ask ourselves how we can overcome them. We will succeed in doing so only if reason and faith come together in a new way, if we overcome the self-imposed limitation of reason to the empirically falsifiable, and if we once more disclose its vast horizons. In this sense theology rightly belongs in the university and within the wide-ranging dialogue of sciences, not merely as a historical discipline and one of the human sciences but precisely as theology, as inquiry into the rationality of faith.

Only thus do we become capable of that genuine dialogue of cultures and religions so urgently needed today. In the Western world it is widely held that only positivistic reason and the forms of philosophy based on it are universally valid. Yet the world's profoundly religious cultures see this exclusion of the divine from the universality of reason as an attack on their most profound convictions. A reason that is deaf to the divine and which relegates religion to the realm of subcultures is incapable of entering into the dialogue of cultures. At the same time, as I have attempted to show, modern scientific reason, with its intrinsically

Platonic element, bears within itself a question that points beyond itself and beyond the possibilities of its methodology. Modern scientific reason quite simply has to accept the rational structure of matter and the correspondence between our spirit and the prevailing rational structures of nature as a given, on which its methodology has to be based. Yet the question why this has to be so is a real question, and one that has to be referred by the natural sciences to other modes and planes of thought – to philosophy and theology. For philosophy and, albeit in a different way, for theology, listening to the great experiences and insights of the religious traditions of humanity, and those of the Christian faith in particular, is a source of knowledge, and to ignore it would be an unacceptable restriction of our listening and responding. Here I am reminded of something Socrates said to Phaedo. In their earlier conversations many false philosophical opinions had been raised, and so Socrates says: 'It would be easily understandable if someone became so annoyed at all these false notions that for the rest of his life he despised and mocked all talk about being – but in this way he would be deprived of the truth of existence and would suffer a great loss.'[13]

The West has long been endangered by this aversion to the questions which underlie its rationality, and can only suffer great harm thereby. The courage to engage the whole breadth of reason, and not the denial of its grandeur – this is the programme with which a theology grounded in biblical faith enters into the debates of our time. 'Not to act reasonably, not to act with *logos*, is contrary to the nature of God,' said Manuel II, according to his Christian understanding of God, in response to his Persian interlocutor. It is to this great *logos*, to this breadth of reason, that we invite our partners in the dialogue of cultures. To rediscover it constantly is the great task of the university.

6

Meeting God by the Use of Reason

Apostolic Journey of his Holiness Benedict XVI to France on the Occasion of the 150th Anniversary of the Apparitions of the Blessed Virgin Mary at Lourdes (12–15 September 2008)

MEETING WITH REPRESENTATIVES FROM THE WORLD OF CULTURE
ADDRESS OF HIS HOLINESS BENEDICT XVI
COLLÈGE DES BERNARDINS, PARIS
FRIDAY, 12 SEPTEMBER 2008

Your Eminence,
Madam Minister of Culture,
Mr Mayor,
Mr Chancellor of the French Institute,
Dear Friends!

I thank you, Your Eminence, for your kind words. We are gathered in a historic place, built by the spiritual sons of St Bernard of Clairvaux, and which your venerable predecessor, the late Cardinal Jean-Marie Lustiger, desired to be a centre of dialogue between Christian wisdom and the cultural, intellectual and artistic currents of contemporary society. In particular, I greet the Minister of Culture, who is here representing the government, together with Mr Giscard d'Estaing and Mr Jacques Chirac. I likewise greet all the ministers present, the representatives of UNESCO, the mayor of Paris and all other authorities in attendance. I do not want to forget my colleagues from the French Institute, who are well aware of my regard for them. I thank the Prince de Broglie for his cordial words. We shall see each other again tomorrow morning. I thank the delegates of the French Islamic community for having accepted the invitation to participate in this meeting: I convey to them by best wishes for the holy season of Ramadan already under way. Of course, I extend warm greetings to the entire, multifaceted world of culture, which you, dear guests, so worthily represent.

I would like to speak with you this evening of the origins of Western theology and the roots of European culture. I begin by recalling that the place in which we are gathered is in a certain way emblematic. It is in fact a place tied to monastic culture, insofar as young monks came to live here in order to learn to understand their vocation more deeply and to be more faithful to their mission. We are in a place that is associated with the culture of monasticism. Does this still have something to say to us today, or are we merely encountering the world of the past?

In order to answer this question, we must consider for a moment the nature of Western monasticism itself. What was it about? From the perspective of monasticism's historical influence, we could say that, amid the great cultural upheaval resulting from migrations of peoples and the emerging new political configurations, the monasteries were the places where the treasures of ancient culture survived, and where at the same time a new culture slowly took shape out of the old. But how did it happen? What motivated men to come together to these places? What did they want? How did they live?

First and foremost, it must be frankly admitted straight away that it was not their intention to create a culture or even to preserve a culture from the past. Their motivation was much more basic. Their goal was: *quaerere Deum*. Amid the confusion of the times, in which nothing seemed permanent, they wanted to do the essential – to make an effort to find what was perennially valid and lasting, life itself. They were searching for God. They wanted to go from the inessential to the essential, to the only truly important and reliable thing there is. It is sometimes said that they were 'eschatologically' oriented. But this is to be understood not in a temporal sense, as if they were looking ahead to the end of the world or to their own death, but in an existential sense: they were seeking the definitive behind the provisional. *Quaerere Deum*: because they were Christians, this was not an expedition into a trackless wilderness, a search leading them into total darkness. God himself had provided signposts; indeed he had marked out a path which was theirs to find and to follow. This path was his word, which had been disclosed to men in the books of the sacred scriptures. Thus, by inner necessity, the search for God demands a culture of the word or – as Jean Leclercq put it – eschatology and grammar are intimately connected with one another in Western monasticism (cf. *L'amour des lettres et le désir de Dieu*). The longing for God, the *désir de Dieu*, includes *amour des lettres*, love of the word, exploration of all its dimensions. Because in the biblical word God comes towards us and we towards him, we must learn to penetrate the secret of language, to understand it in its construction and in the manner of its expression. Thus it is through the search for God that the secular sciences take on their importance, sciences which show us the path towards language. Because the search for God required the culture of the word, it was appropriate that the monastery should have a library, pointing out pathways to the word. It was also appropriate to have a school, in which these pathways could be opened up. Benedict calls the monastery a *dominici servitii schola*. The monastery serves *eruditio*, the formation and education of man – a formation whose ultimate aim is that man should learn how to serve God. But it also includes the formation of reason – education – through which man learns to perceive, in the midst of words, the Word itself.

Yet in order to have a full vision of the culture of the Word, which essentially pertains to the search for God, we must take a further step. The Word which opens the path of that search, and is to be identified with this path, is a shared word. True, it pierces every individual to the heart (cf. Acts 2.37). Gregory the Great describes this as a sharp stabbing pain, which tears open our sleeping soul and awakens us, making us attentive to the essential reality, to God.[1] But in the process, it also makes us attentive to one another. The Word leads not to a purely individual path of mystical immersion, but to the pilgrim fellowship of faith. And so this word must be not only pondered, but also correctly read. As in the rabbinic schools, so too with the monks, reading by the individual is at the same time a corporate activity. 'But if *legere* and *lectio* are used without an explanatory note, then they designate for the most part an activity which, like singing and writing, engages the whole body and the whole spirit', says Jean Leclercq on the subject.[2]

And once again, a further step is needed. We ourselves are brought into conversation with God by the word of God. The God who speaks in the Bible teaches us how to speak with him ourselves. Particularly in the book of Psalms, he gives us the words with which we can address him, with which we can bring our life, with all its high points and low points, into conversation with him, so that life itself thereby becomes a movement towards him.

The Psalms also contain frequent instructions about how they should be sung and accompanied by instruments. For prayer that issues from the word of God, speech is not enough: music is required. Two chants from the Christian liturgy come from biblical texts in which they are placed on the lips of angels: the Gloria, which is sung by the angels at the birth of Jesus, and the Sanctus, which according to Isaiah 6 is the cry of the seraphim who stand directly before God. Christian worship is therefore an invitation to sing with the angels, and thus to lead the word to its highest destination. Once again, Jean Leclercq says on this subject: 'The monks had to find melodies which translate into music the acceptance by redeemed man of the mysteries that he celebrates. The few surviving *capitula* from Cluny thus show the Christological symbols of the individual modes.'[3]

For Benedict, the words of the Psalm '*coram angelis psallam Tibi, Domine*' – 'in the presence of the angels, I will sing your praise' (cf. Ps. 138.1) – are the decisive rule governing the prayer and chant of the monks. What this expresses is the awareness that in communal prayer one is singing in the presence of the entire heavenly court, and is thereby measured according to the very highest standards, that one is praying and singing in such a way as to harmonize with the music of the noble spirits who were considered the originators of the harmony of the cosmos, the music of the spheres. From this perspective one can understand the seriousness of a remark by St Bernard of Clairvaux, who used an expression from the Platonic tradition handed down by Augustine, to pass judgement on the poor singing of monks, which for him was evidently very far from being a mishap of only minor importance. He describes the confusion resulting from a poorly executed chant as a falling into the 'zone of dissimilarity' – the *regio dissimilitudinis*. Augustine had borrowed this phrase from Platonic philosophy, in order to designate his condition prior to conversion (cf. *Confessions,* VII, 10.16): man, who is created in God's likeness, falls in his godforsakenness into the 'zone of dissimilarity' – into a remoteness from God, in which he no longer reflects him, and so has become dissimilar not only to God but to himself, to what being human truly is.

Bernard is certainly putting it strongly when he uses this phrase, which indicates man's falling away from himself, to describe bad singing by monks. But it shows how seriously he viewed the matter. It shows that the culture of singing is also the culture of being, and that the monks have to pray and sing in a manner commensurate with the grandeur of the word handed down to them, with its claim on true beauty. This intrinsic requirement of speaking with God and singing of him with words he himself has given is what gave rise to the great tradition of Western music. It was not a form of private 'creativity', in which the individual leaves a memorial to himself and makes self-representation his essential criterion. Rather, it is about vigilantly recognizing with the 'ears of the heart' the inner laws of the music of creation, the archetypes of music that the Creator built into his world and into men, and thus discovering music that is worthy of God, and at the same time truly worthy of man, music whose worthiness resounds in purity.

In order to understand to some degree the culture of the word, which developed deep within Western monasticism from the search for God, we need to touch at least briefly on the particular character of the book, or rather books, in which the monks encountered this word. The Bible, considered from a purely historical and literary perspective, is not simply a book but a collection of literary texts which were redacted over the course of more than a thousand years, and in which the inner unity of the individual books is not immediately apparent. Indeed, there are visible tensions between them. This is already the case within the Bible of Israel, which we Christians call the Old Testament. It is only rectified when we as Christians link the New Testament writings as, so to speak, a hermeneutical key with the Bible of Israel, and so understand the latter as the journey towards Christ. With good reason, the New Testament generally designates the Bible not as 'the Scripture' but as 'the Scriptures', which, when taken together, are naturally then regarded as the one word of God to us. But the use of this plural makes it quite clear that the word of God only comes to us through the human word and through human words, that God only speaks to us through the humanity of human agents, through their words and their history. This means again that the divine element in the word and in the words is not self-evident.

To put this in a modern way: the unity of the biblical books and the divine character of their words cannot be grasped by purely historical methods. The historical element is seen in the multiplicity and the humanity. From this perspective one can understand the formulation of a medieval couplet that at first sight appears rather disconcerting: *littera gesta docet – quid credas allegoria ...* (cf. Augustine of Dacia, *Rotulus pugillaris,* I). The letter indicates the facts; what you have to believe is indicated by allegory: that is to say, by Christological and pneumatological exegesis.

We may put it even more simply: scripture requires exegesis, and it requires the context of the community in which it came to birth and in which it is lived. This is where its unity is to be found, and here too its unifying meaning is opened up. To put it yet another way: there are dimensions of meaning in the word and in words which only come to light within the living community of this history-generating word. Through the growing realization of the different layers of meaning the word is not devalued, but in fact appears in its full grandeur and dignity. Therefore the Catechism of the Catholic Church can rightly say that Christianity does not simply represent a religion of the book in the classical sense (cf. para. 108). It perceives in the words *the* Word, the *Logos* itself, which spreads its mystery through this multiplicity and the reality of a human history.

This particular structure of the Bible issues a constantly new challenge to every generation. It excludes by its nature everything that today is known as fundamentalism. In effect, the word of God can never simply be equated with the letter of the text. To attain to it involves a transcending and a process of understanding, led by the inner movement of the whole, and hence it also has to become a process of living. Only within the dynamic unity of the whole are the many books *one* book. The Word of God and his action in the world are revealed only in the word and history of human beings.

The whole drama of this topic is illuminated in the writings of St Paul. What is meant by the transcending of the letter and understanding it solely from the perspective of the whole he forcefully expressed as follows: 'The letter kills, but the Spirit gives life' (2 Cor. 3.6). And he continues: 'Where the Spirit is ... there is freedom' (cf. 2 Cor. 3.17). But one can only understand the greatness and breadth of this vision of the biblical word if one listens closely to Paul and then discovers that this liberating Spirit has a name, and hence that freedom has an inner criterion: 'The Lord is the Spirit. Where the Spirit is ... there is freedom' (2 Cor. 3.17). The liberating Spirit is not simply the exegete's own idea, the exegete's own vision. The Spirit is Christ, and Christ is the Lord who shows us the way.

With the word of Spirit and of freedom, a further horizon opens up, but at the same time a clear limit is placed on arbitrariness and subjectivity, which unequivocally binds both the individual and the community and brings about a new, higher obligation than that of the letter: namely, the obligation of insight and love. This tension between obligation and freedom, which extends far beyond the literary problem of scriptural exegesis, has also determined the thinking and acting of monasticism and has deeply marked Western culture. This tension presents itself anew as a challenge for our own generation as we face two poles: on the one hand, subjective arbitrariness, and on the other, fundamentalist fanaticism. It would be a disaster if today's European culture could only conceive freedom as absence of obligation, which would inevitably play into the hands of fanaticism and arbitrariness. Absence of obligation and arbitrariness signify not freedom but its destruction.

Thus far in our consideration of the 'school of God's service', as Benedict describes monasticism, we have examined only its orientation towards the word – towards the *ora*. Indeed, this is the starting point that sets the direction for the entire monastic life. But our consideration would remain incomplete if we did not also at least briefly glance at the second component of monasticism, indicated by the *labora*. In the Greek world, manual labour was considered something for slaves. Only the wise man, the one who is truly free, devotes himself to the things of the spirit; he views manual labour as somehow beneath him, and leaves it to people who are not suited to this higher existence in the world of the spirit. The Jewish tradition was quite different: all the great rabbis practised at the same time some form of handcraft. Paul, who as a rabbi and then as a preacher of the Gospel to the Gentile world was also a tent-maker and earned his living with the work of his own hands, is no exception here, but stands within the common tradition of the rabbinate. Monasticism took up this tradition; manual work is a constitutive element of Christian monasticism. In his *Regula,* St Benedict does not speak specifically about schools, although in practice he presupposes teaching and learning, as we have seen. However, in one chapter of his Rule, he does speak explicitly about work (cf. Chap. 48). And so does Augustine, who dedicated a book of his own to monastic work. Christians, who thus continued in the tradition previously established by Judaism, must have felt further vindicated by Jesus' saying in St John's Gospel, in defence of his activity on the Sabbath: 'My Father is working still, and I am working' (Jn 5.17). The Graeco-Roman world did not have a creator God; according to its vision, the highest divinity could not, as it were, dirty his hands in the business of creating matter. The 'making' of the world was the work of the Demiurge, a lower deity. The Christian God is different: he, the one, real and only God, is also the creator.

God is working; he continues working in and on human history. In Christ he enters personally into the laborious work of history. 'My Father is working still, and I am working.' God himself is the creator of the world, and creation is not yet finished. God works, *ergázetai*! Thus human work was now seen as a special form of human resemblance to God, as a way in which man can and may share in God's activity as creator of the world. Monasticism involves not only a culture of the word but also a culture of work, without which the emergence of Europe, its ethos and its influence on the world would be unthinkable. Naturally, this ethos had to include the idea that human work and shaping of history is understood as sharing in the work of the creator, and must be evaluated in those terms. Where such evaluation is lacking, where man arrogates to himself the status of god-like creator, his shaping of the world can quickly turn into destruction of the world.

We set out from the premise that the basic attitude of monks in the face of the collapse of the old order and its certainties was *quaerere Deum* – setting out in search of God. We could describe this as the truly philosophical attitude: looking beyond the penultimate, and setting out in search of the ultimate and the true. By becoming a monk, a man set out on a broad and noble path, but he had already found the direction he needed: the word of the Bible, in which he heard God himself speaking. Now he had to try to understand him, so as to be able to approach him. So the monastic journey is indeed a journey into the inner world of the received word, even if an infinite distance is involved. Within the monks' seeking there is already contained, in some respects, a finding. Therefore, if such seeking is to be possible at all, there has to be an initial spur, which not only arouses the will to seek but also makes it possible to believe that the way is concealed within this word, or rather, that in this word God himself has set out towards men, and hence men can come to God through it.

To put it another way: there must be proclamation, which speaks to man and so creates conviction, which in turn can become life. If a way is to be opened up into the heart of the biblical word as God's word, this word must first of all be proclaimed outwardly. The classic formulation of the Christian faith's intrinsic need to make itself communicable to others is a phrase from the First Letter of Peter, which in medieval theology was regarded as the biblical basis for the work of theologians: 'Always have your answer ready for people who ask you the reason (the *logos*) for the hope that you all have' (1 Pet. 3.15). (The *Logos*, the reason for hope must become *apo-logía*; it must become a response.) In fact, Christians of the nascent Church regarded their missionary proclamation not as propaganda, designed to enlarge their particular group, but as an inner necessity, consequent on the nature of their faith: the God in whom they believed was the God of all people, the one, true God, who had revealed himself in the history of Israel and ultimately in his Son, thereby supplying the answer which was of concern to everyone and for which all people, in their innermost hearts, are waiting. The universality of God, and of reason open towards him, is what gave them the motivation – indeed, the obligation – to proclaim the message. They saw their faith as belonging not to cultural custom, which differs from one people to another, but to the domain of truth, which concerns all people equally.

The fundamental structure of Christian proclamation 'outwards' – towards searching and questioning mankind – is seen in St Paul's address at the Areopagus. We should remember that the Areopagus was not a form of academy, at which the most illustrious minds would meet for discussion of lofty matters, but a court of justice, which was competent in matters of religion and ought to have opposed the import of foreign religions. This is exactly what Paul is reproached for: 'he seems to be a preacher of foreign divinities' (Acts 17.18). To this Paul responds: I have found an altar of yours with this inscription: 'to an unknown god'. What therefore you worship as unknown, this I proclaim to you (Acts 17.23). Paul is not proclaiming unknown gods. He is proclaiming him whom men do not know and yet do know – the unknown-known; the one they are seeking, whom ultimately they know already and who yet remains unknown and unrecognizable. The deepest layer of human thinking and feeling somehow knows that he must exist, that at the beginning of all things there must be not irrationality but creative reason – not blind chance but freedom. Yet even though all men somehow know this, as Paul expressly says in the Letter to the Romans (Rom. 1:21), this knowledge remains unreal: a God who is merely imagined and invented is not God at all. If he does not reveal himself, we cannot gain access to him.

The novelty of Christian proclamation is that it can now say to all peoples: he has revealed himself. He personally. And now the way to him is open. The novelty of Christian proclamation consists not in a thought but in a deed: God has revealed himself. Yet this is no blind deed but one which is itself *Logos* – the presence of eternal reason in our flesh. *Verbum caro factum est* (Jn 1.14): just so, amid what is made (*factum*) there is now *Logos*, *Logos* is among us. Creation (*factum*) is rational. Naturally, the humility of reason is always needed, in order to accept it: man's humility, which responds to God's humility.

Our present situation differs in many respects from the one that Paul encountered in Athens, yet the two situations also have much in common. Our cities are no longer filled with altars and with images of multiple deities. God has truly become for many the great unknown. But just as in the past, when behind the many images of God the question concerning the unknown God was hidden and present, so too the present absence of God is silently besieged by the question concerning him. *Quaerere Deum* – to seek God and to let oneself be found by him – that is today no less necessary than in former times. A purely positivistic culture which tried to drive the question concerning God into the subjective realm, as being unscientific, would be the capitulation of reason, the renunciation of its highest possibilities, and hence a disaster for humanity, with very grave consequences. What gave Europe's culture its foundation – the search for God and the readiness to listen to him – remains today the basis of any genuine culture.

Thank you.

7

Religion Is Vital for Society

Conclusion of the Year for Priests
Holy Mass

HOMILY OF HIS HOLINESS POPE
BENEDICT XVI
SOLEMNITY OF THE SACRED HEART OF
JESUS ST PETER'S SQUARE
FRIDAY, 11 JUNE 2010

Dear Brothers in the Priestly Ministry,
Dear Brothers and Sisters,

The Year for Priests which we have celebrated on the 150th anniversary of the death of the holy Curé of Ars, the model of priestly ministry in our world, is now coming to an end. We have let the Curé of Ars guide us to a renewed appreciation of the grandeur and beauty of the priestly ministry. The priest is not a mere office-holder, like those which every society needs in order to carry out certain functions. Instead, he does something which no human being can do of his own power: in Christ's name he speaks the words which absolve us of our sins, and in this way he changes, starting with God, our entire life. Over the offerings of bread and wine he speaks Christ's words of thanksgiving, which are words of transubstantiation – words that make Christ himself present, the risen one, his body and blood – words that thus transform the elements of the world, which open the world to God and unite it to him.

The priesthood, then, is not simply 'office' but sacrament: God makes use of us poor men in order to be, through us, present to all men and women, and to act on their behalf. This audacity of God who entrusts himself to human beings – who, conscious of our weaknesses, nonetheless considers men capable of acting and being present in his stead – this audacity of God is the true grandeur concealed in the word 'priesthood'. That God thinks that we are capable of this, that in this way he calls men to his service and thus from within binds himself to them, this is what we wanted to reflect on and appreciate anew over the course of the past year. We wanted to reawaken our joy at how close God is to us, and our gratitude for the fact that he entrusts himself to our infirmities, that he guides and sustains us daily.

In this way we also wanted to demonstrate once again to young people that this vocation, this fellowship of service for God and with God, does exist – and that God is indeed waiting for us to say 'yes'. Together with the whole Church we wanted to make clear once again that we have to ask God for this vocation. We have to beg for workers for God's harvest, and this petition to God is, at the same time, his own way of knocking on the hearts of young people who consider themselves able to do what God considers them able to do. It was to be expected that this new radiance of the priesthood would not be pleasing to the 'enemy'; he would have rather preferred to see it disappear, so that God would ultimately be driven out of the world. And so it happened that, in this very year of joy for the sacrament of the priesthood, the sins of priests came to light – particularly the abuse of the little ones, in which the priesthood, whose task is to manifest God's concern for our good, turns into its very opposite. We too insistently beg forgiveness from God and from the persons involved, while promising to do everything possible to ensure that such abuse will never occur again and that, in admitting men to priestly ministry and in their formation, we will do everything we can to weigh the authenticity of their vocation and make every effort to accompany priests along their journey, so that the Lord will protect them and watch over them in troubled situations and amid life's dangers.

Had the Year for Priests been a glorification of our individual human performance, it would have been ruined by these events. But for us what happened was precisely the opposite: we grew in gratitude for God's gift, a gift concealed in 'earthen vessels' which ever anew, even amid human weakness, makes his love concretely present in this world. So let us look upon all that happened as a summons to purification, as a task that we bring to the future and which makes us acknowledge and love all the more the great gift we have received from God. In this way, his gift becomes a commitment to respond to God's courage and humility by our own courage and our own humility. The word of God, which we have sung in the Entrance Antiphon of the liturgy, can speak to us, at this hour, of what it means to become and to be priests: 'Take my yoke upon you, and learn from me; for I am gentle and humble of heart' (Mt. 11.29).

We are celebrating the feast of the Sacred Heart of Jesus, and in the liturgy we peer, as it were, into the heart of Jesus opened in death by the spear of the Roman soldier. Jesus' heart was indeed opened for us and before us – and thus God's own heart was opened. The liturgy interprets for us the language of Jesus' heart, which tells us above all that God is the shepherd of mankind, and so it reveals to us Jesus' priesthood, which is rooted deep within his heart; so too it shows us the perennial foundation and the effective criterion of all priestly ministry, which must always be anchored in the heart of Jesus and lived out from that starting point.

Today I would like to meditate especially on those texts with which the Church in prayer responds to the word of God presented in the readings. In those chants, word (*Wort*) and response (*Ant wort*) interpenetrate. On the one hand the chants are themselves drawn from the word of God, yet on the other they are already our human response to that word, a response in which the word itself is communicated and enters into our lives. The most important of those texts in today's liturgy is Psalm 23 – 'The Lord is my shepherd' – in which Israel at prayer received God's self-revelation as shepherd, and made this the guide of its own life. 'The Lord is my shepherd, I shall not want': this first verse expresses joy and gratitude for the fact that God is present to and concerned for us.

The reading from the Book of Ezekiel begins with the same theme: 'I myself will look after and tend my sheep' (Ezek. 34.11). God personally looks after me, after us, after all mankind. I am not abandoned, adrift in the universe and in a society which leaves me ever more lost and bewildered. God looks after me. He is not a distant God, for whom my life is worthless. The world's religions, as far as we can see, have always known that in the end there is only one God. But this God was distant. Evidently he had abandoned the world to other powers and forces, to other divinities. It was with these that one had to deal. The one God was good, but aloof. He was not dangerous, but nor was he very helpful. Consequently one didn't need to worry about him. He did not lord it over us. Oddly, this kind of thinking re-emerged during the Enlightenment. There was still a recognition that the world presupposes a Creator. Yet this God, after making the world, had evidently withdrawn from it. The world itself had a certain set of laws by which it ran, and God did not, could not, intervene in them. God was only a remote cause.

Many perhaps did not even want God to look after them. They did not want God to get in the way. But wherever God's loving concern is perceived as getting in the way, human beings go awry. It is fine and consoling to know that there is someone who loves me and looks after me. But it is far more important that there is a God who knows me, loves me and is concerned about me. 'I know my own and my own know me' (Jn 10.14), the Church says before the Gospel with the Lord's words. God knows me, he is concerned about me. This thought should make us truly joyful. Let us allow it to penetrate the depths of our being.

Then let us also realize what it means: God wants us, as priests, in one tiny moment of history, to share his concern for people. As priests, we want to be persons who share his concern for men and women, who take care of them and provide them with a concrete experience of God's concern. Whatever the field of activity entrusted to him, the priest, with the Lord, ought to be able to say: 'I know my sheep and mine know me.' 'To know', in the idiom of sacred Scripture, never refers to merely exterior knowledge, like the knowledge of someone's telephone number. 'Knowing' means being inwardly close to another person. It means loving him or her. We should strive to 'know' men and women as God does and for God's sake; we should strive to walk with them along the path of God's friendship.

Let us return to our Psalm. There we read: 'He leads me in right paths for his name's sake. Even though I walk through the darkest valley, I fear no evil; for you are with me; your rod and your staff – they comfort me' (Ps. 23.3ff.). The shepherd points out the right path to those entrusted to him. He goes before them and leads them. Let us put it differently: the Lord shows us the right way to be human. He teaches us the art of being a person. What must I do in order not to fall, not to squander my life in meaninglessness? This is precisely the question that every man and woman must ask, and one that remains valid at every moment of one's life. How much darkness surrounds this question in our own day! We are constantly reminded of the words of Jesus, who felt compassion for the crowds because they were like a flock without a shepherd. Lord, have mercy on us too! Show us the way! From the Gospel we know this much: he is himself the way. Living with Christ, following him – this means finding the right way, so that our lives can be meaningful and so that one day we might say: 'Yes, it was good to have lived.' The people of Israel continue to be grateful to God because in the Commandments he pointed out the way of life.

The great Psalm 119 is a unique expression of joy for this fact: we are not fumbling in the dark. God has shown us the way and how to walk aright. The message of the Commandments was synthesized in the life of Jesus and became a living model. Thus we understand that these rules from God are not chains, but the way which he is pointing out to us. We can be glad for them and rejoice that in Christ they stand before us as a lived reality. He himself has made us glad. By walking with Christ, we experience the joy of Revelation, and as priests we need to communicate to others our own joy at the fact that we have been shown the right way of life.

Then there is the phrase about the 'darkest valley' through which the Lord leads us. Our path as individuals will one day lead us into the valley of the shadow of death, where no one can accompany us. Yet he will be there. Christ himself descended into the dark night of death. Even there he will not abandon us. Even there he will lead us. 'If I sink to the nether world, you are present there,' says Psalm 139. Truly you are there, even in the throes of death, and hence our Responsorial Psalm can say: even there, in the darkest valley, I fear no evil. When speaking of the darkest valley, we can also think of the dark valleys of temptation, discouragement and trial through which everyone has to pass. Even in these dark valleys of life he is there. Lord, in the darkness of temptation, at the hour of dusk when all light seems to have died away, show me that you are there. Help us priests, so that we can remain beside the persons entrusted to us in these dark nights. So that we can show them your own light.

'Your rod and your staff – they comfort me': the shepherd needs the rod as protection against savage beasts ready to pounce on the flock; against robbers looking for prey. Along with the rod there is the staff which gives support and helps to make difficult crossings. Both of these are likewise part of the Church's ministry, of the priest's ministry. The Church too must use the shepherd's rod, the rod with which he protects the faith against those who falsify it, against currents which lead the flock astray. The use of the rod can actually be a service of love. Today we can see that it has nothing to do with love when conduct unworthy of the priestly life is tolerated. Nor does it have to do with love if heresy is allowed to spread and the faith twisted and chipped away, as if it were something that we ourselves had invented. As if it were no longer God's gift, the precious pearl which we cannot let be taken from us. Even so, the rod must always become once again the shepherd's staff – a staff that helps men and women to tread difficult paths and to follow the Lord.

At the end of the Psalm we read of the table which is set, the oil which anoints the head, the cup which overflows and dwelling in the house of the Lord. In the Psalm this is an expression first and foremost of the prospect of the festal joy of being in God's presence in the temple, of being his guest, whom he himself serves, of dwelling with him. For us, who pray this Psalm with Christ and his Body which is the Church, this prospect of hope takes on even greater breadth and depth. We see in these words a kind of prophetic foreshadowing of the mystery of the Eucharist, in which God himself makes us his guests and offers himself to us as food – as that bread and fine wine which alone can definitively sate man's hunger and thirst. How can we not rejoice that one day we will be guests at the very table of God and live in his dwelling-place? How can we not rejoice at the fact that he has commanded us, 'Do this in memory of me'? How can we not rejoice that he has enabled us to set God's table for men and women, to give them his Body and his Blood, to offer them the precious gift of his very presence. Truly we can pray together, with all our heart, the words of the Psalm: 'Goodness and mercy shall follow me all the days of my life' (Ps. 23.6).

Finally, let us take a brief look at the two Communion Antiphons which the Church offers us in her liturgy today. First there are the words with which St John concludes the account of Jesus' crucifixion: 'One of the soldiers pierced his side with a spear, and at once blood and water came out' (Jn 19.34). The heart of Jesus is pierced by the spear. Once opened, it becomes a fountain:

the water and the blood which stream forth recall the two fundamental sacraments by which the Church lives: baptism and the Eucharist. From the Lord's pierced side, from his open heart, there springs the living fountain which continues to well up over the centuries and which makes the Church. The open heart is the source of a new stream of life; here John was certainly also thinking of the prophecy of Ezekiel, who saw flowing forth from the new temple a torrent bestowing fruitfulness and life (Ezek. 47): Jesus himself is the new temple, and his open heart is the source of a stream of new life which is communicated to us in baptism and the Eucharist.

The liturgy of the Solemnity of the Sacred Heart of Jesus also permits another phrase, similar to this, to be used as the Communion Antiphon. It is taken from the Gospel of John: Whoever is thirsty, let him come to me. And let the one who believes in me drink. As the Scripture has said: 'Out of his heart shall flow rivers of living water' (cf. Jn 7.37ff.) In faith we drink, so to speak, of the living water of God's Word. In this way the believer himself becomes a wellspring which gives living water to the parched earth of history. We see this in the saints. We see this in Mary, that great woman of faith and love who has become in every generation a wellspring of faith, love and life.

Every Christian and every priest should become, starting from Christ, a wellspring which gives life to others. We ought to be offering life-giving water to a parched and thirsty world.

Lord, we thank you because for our sake you opened your heart; because in your death and in your resurrection you became the source of life. Give us life, make us live from you as our source, and grant that we too may be sources, wellsprings capable of bestowing the water of life in our time. We thank you for the grace of the priestly ministry. Lord bless us, and bless all those who in our time are thirsty and continue to seek. Amen.

I now wish to greet all the English-speaking priests present at today's celebration! My dear brothers, as I thank you for your love of Christ and of his bride the Church, I ask you again solemnly to be faithful to your promises. Serve God and your people with holiness and courage, and always conform your lives to the mystery of the Lord's cross. May God bless your apostolic labours abundantly!

8

The Priest Bears Witness to God's Mercy

Apostolic Journey to the United Kingdom
(16–19 September 2010)
Meeting with the Representatives of British
Society, Including the Diplomatic Corps,
Politicians, Academics and Business Leaders

ADDRESS OF HIS HOLINESS
BENEDICT XVI
WESTMINSTER HALL, CITY
OF WESTMINSTER FRIDAY,
17 SEPTEMBER 2010[1]

Mr Speaker,

Thank you for your words of welcome on behalf of this distinguished gathering. As I address you, I am conscious of the privilege afforded me to speak to the British people and their representatives in Westminster Hall, a building of unique significance in the civil and political history of the people of these islands.

Allow me also to express my esteem for the Parliament which has existed on this site for centuries and which has had such a profound influence on the development of participative government among the nations, especially in the Commonwealth and the English-speaking world at large. Your common-law tradition serves as the basis of legal systems in many parts of the world, and your particular vision of the respective rights and duties of the state and the individual, and of the separation of powers, remains an inspiration to many across the globe.

As I speak to you in this historic setting, I think of the countless men and women down the centuries who have played their part in the momentous events that have taken place within these walls and have shaped the lives of many generations of Britons, and others besides. In particular, I recall the figure of St Thomas More, the great English scholar and statesman, who is admired by believers and non-believers alike for the integrity with which he followed his conscience, even at the cost of displeasing the sovereign whose 'good servant' he was, because he chose to serve God first. The dilemma which faced More in those difficult times, the perennial question of the relationship between what is owed to Caesar and what is owed to God, allows me the opportunity to reflect with you briefly on the proper place of religious belief within the political process.

This country's Parliamentary tradition owes much to the national instinct for moderation, to the desire to achieve a genuine balance between the legitimate claims of government and the rights of those subject to it. While decisive steps have been taken at several points in your history to place limits on the exercise of power, the nation's political institutions have been able to evolve with a remarkable degree of stability. In the process, Britain has emerged as a pluralist democracy which places great value on freedom of speech, freedom of political affiliation and respect for the rule of law, with a strong sense of the individual's rights and duties, and of the equality of all citizens before the law. While couched in different language, Catholic social teaching has much in common with this approach, in its overriding concern to safeguard the unique dignity of every human person, created in the image and likeness of God, and in its emphasis on the duty of civil authority to foster the common good.

And yet the fundamental questions at stake in Thomas More's trial continue to present themselves in ever-changing terms as new social conditions emerge. Each generation, as it seeks to advance the common good, must ask anew: what are the requirements that governments may reasonably impose on citizens, and how far do they extend? By appeal to what authority can moral dilemmas be resolved? These questions take us directly to the ethical foundations of civil discourse. If the moral principles underpinning the democratic process are themselves determined by nothing more solid than social consensus, then the fragility of the process becomes all too evident – herein lies the real challenge for democracy.

The inadequacy of pragmatic, short-term solutions to complex social and ethical problems has been illustrated all too clearly by the recent global financial crisis. There is widespread agreement that the lack of a solid ethical foundation for economic activity has contributed to the grave difficulties now being experienced by millions of people throughout the world. Just as 'every economic decision has a moral consequence' (*Caritas in Veritate*, 37), so too in the political field the ethical dimension of policy has far-reaching consequences that no government can afford to ignore. A positive illustration of this is found in one of the British Parliament's particularly notable achievements – the abolition of the slave trade. The campaign that led to this landmark legislation was built on firm ethical principles, rooted in the natural law, and it has made a contribution to civilization of which this nation may be justly proud.

The central question at issue, then, is this: where is the ethical foundation for political choices to be found? The Catholic tradition maintains that the objective norms governing right action are accessible to reason, prescinding from the content of revelation. According to this understanding, the role of religion in political debate is not so much to supply these norms, as if they could not be known by non-believers – still less to propose concrete political solutions, which would lie altogether outside the competence of religion – but rather to help purify and shed light on the application of reason to the discovery of objective moral principles. This 'corrective' role of religion vis-à-vis reason is not always welcomed, though, partly because distorted forms of religion, such as sectarianism and fundamentalism, can be seen to create serious social problems themselves. And in their turn, these distortions of religion arise when insufficient attention is given to the purifying and structuring role of reason within religion. It is a two-way process.

Without the corrective supplied by religion, though, reason too can fall prey to distortions, as when it is manipulated by ideology, or applied in a partial way that fails to take full account of the dignity of the human person. Such misuse of reason, after all, was what gave rise to the slave trade in the first place and to many other social evils, not least the totalitarian ideologies of the twentieth century. This is why I would suggest that the world of reason and the world of faith – the world of secular rationality and the world of religious belief – need one another and should not be afraid to enter into a profound and ongoing dialogue, for the good of our civilization.

Religion, in other words, is not a problem for legislators to solve but a vital contributor to the national conversation. In this light I cannot but voice my concern at the increasing marginalization of religion, particularly of Christianity, that is taking place in some quarters, even in nations that place a great emphasis on tolerance. There are those who would advocate that the voice of religion be silenced, or at least relegated to the purely private sphere. There are those who argue that the public celebration of festivals such as Christmas should be discouraged, in the questionable belief that it might somehow offend those of other religions or none. And there are those who argue – paradoxically with the intention of eliminating discrimination – that Christians in public roles should be required at times to act against their conscience.

These are worrying signs of a failure to appreciate not only the rights of believers to freedom of conscience and freedom of religion but also the legitimate role of religion in the public square. I would invite all of you, therefore, within your respective spheres of influence, to seek ways of promoting and encouraging dialogue between faith and reason at every level of national life.

Your readiness to do so is already implied in the unprecedented invitation extended to me today. And it finds expression in the fields of concern in which your government has been engaged with the Holy See. In the area of peace, there have been exchanges regarding the elaboration of an international arms trade treaty; regarding human rights, the Holy See and the United Kingdom have welcomed the spread of democracy, especially in the last sixty-five years; in the field of development, there has been collaboration on debt relief, fair trade and financing for development, particularly through the International Finance Facility, the International Immunization Bond and the Advanced Market Commitment. The Holy See also looks forward to exploring with the United Kingdom new ways to promote environmental responsibility, to the benefit of all.

I also note that the present government has committed the United Kingdom to devoting 0.7 per cent of national income to development aid by 2013. In recent years it has been encouraging to witness the positive signs of a worldwide growth in solidarity towards the poor. But to turn this solidarity into effective action calls for fresh thinking that will improve life conditions in many important areas, such as food production, clean water, job creation, education, support to families, especially migrants, and basic healthcare. Where human lives are concerned, time is always short: yet the world has witnessed the vast resources that governments can draw on to rescue financial institutions deemed 'too big to fail'. Surely the integral human development of the world's peoples is no less important: here is an enterprise, worthy of the world's attention, that is truly 'too big to fail'.

This overview of recent cooperation between the United Kingdom and the Holy See illustrates well how much progress has been made, in the years that have passed since the establishment of bilateral diplomatic relations, in promoting throughout the world the many core values that we share. I hope and pray that this relationship will continue to bear fruit, and that it will be mirrored in a growing acceptance of the need for dialogue and respect at every level of society between the world of reason and the world of faith. I am convinced that, within this country too, there are many areas in which the Church and the public authorities can work together for the good of citizens, in harmony with this Parliament's historic practice of invoking the Spirit's guidance on those who seek to improve the conditions of all mankind. For such cooperation to be possible, religious bodies – including institutions linked to the Catholic Church – need to be free to act in accordance with their own principles and specific convictions based on the faith and the official teaching of the Church. In this way such basic rights as religious freedom, freedom of conscience and freedom of association are guaranteed.

The angels looking down on us from the magnificent ceiling of this ancient Hall remind us of the long tradition from which British Parliamentary democracy has evolved. They remind us that God is constantly watching over us to guide and protect us. And they summon us to acknowledge the vital contribution that religious belief has made and can continue to make to the life of the nation.

Mr Speaker, I thank you once again for this opportunity briefly to address this distinguished audience. Let me assure you and the Lord Speaker of my continued good wishes and prayers for you and for the fruitful work of both Houses of this ancient Parliament. Thank you and God bless you all!

9

With God Human Rights
Are Assured

Apostolic Journey to Germany 22–5 September
2011
Visit to the Bundestag

ADDRESS OF HIS HOLINESS BENEDICT
XVI
REICHSTAG BUILDING, BERLIN
THURSDAY, 22 SEPTEMBER 2011

Mr President of the Federal Republic,
Mr President of the Bundestag,
Madam Chancellor,
Madam President of the Bundesrat,
Ladies and Gentlemen Members of the House,

It is an honour and a joy for me to speak before this distinguished house, before the Parliament of my native Germany, which meets here as a democratically elected representation of the people, in order to work for the good of the Federal Republic of Germany. I should like to thank the President of the Bundestag both for his invitation to deliver this address and for the kind words of greeting and appreciation with which he has welcomed me. At this moment I turn to you, distinguished ladies and gentlemen, not least as your fellow-countryman who for all his life has been conscious of close links to his origins, and has followed the affairs of his native Germany with keen interest. But the invitation to give this address was extended to me as pope, as the bishop of Rome, who bears the highest responsibility for Catholic Christianity. In issuing this invitation you are acknowledging the role that the Holy See plays as a partner within the community of peoples and states. Setting out from this international responsibility that I hold, I should like to propose to you some thoughts on the foundations of a free state of law.

Allow me to begin my reflections on the foundations of law [*Recht*] with a brief story from sacred scripture. In the First Book of the Kings it is recounted that God invited the young King

Solomon, on his accession to the throne, to make a request. What will the young ruler ask for at this important moment? Success? Wealth? Long life? Destruction of his enemies? He chooses none of these things. Instead, he asks for a listening heart so that he may govern God's people, and discern between good and evil (cf. 1 Kgs 3.9). Through this story, the Bible wants to tell us what should ultimately matter for a politician. Their fundamental criterion and the motivation for their work as a politician must not be success, and certainly not material gain. Politics must be a striving for justice, and hence it has to establish the fundamental preconditions for peace. Naturally a politician will seek success, without which they would have no opportunity for effective political action at all. Yet success is subordinated to the criterion of justice, to the will to do what is right and to the understanding of what is right. Success can also be seductive and thus can open up the path towards the falsification of what is right, towards the destruction of justice. 'Without justice – what else is the State but a great band of robbers?', as St Augustine once said.

We Germans know from our own experience that these words are no empty spectre. We have seen how power became divorced from right, how power opposed right and crushed it, so that the state became an instrument for destroying right – a highly organized band of robbers, capable of threatening the whole world and driving it to the edge of the abyss. To serve right and to fight against the dominion of wrong is and remains the fundamental task of the politician. At a moment in history when man has acquired previously inconceivable power, this task takes on a particular urgency. Man can destroy the world. He can manipulate himself. He can, so to speak, make human beings and he can deny them their humanity. How do we recognize what is right? How can we discern between good and evil, between what is truly right and what may appear right? Even now, Solomon's request remains the decisive issue facing politicians and politics today.

For most of the matters that need to be regulated by law, the support of the majority can serve as a sufficient criterion. Yet it is evident that for the fundamental issues of law, in which the dignity of man and of humanity is at stake, the majority principle is not enough: everyone in a position of responsibility must personally seek out the criteria to be followed when framing laws. In the third century the great theologian Origen provided the following explanation for the resistance of Christians to certain legal systems: 'Suppose that a man were living among the Scythians, whose laws are contrary to the divine law, and was compelled to live among them ... such a man for the sake of the true law, though illegal among the Scythians, would rightly form associations with like-minded people contrary to the laws of the Scythians.'[1]

This conviction was what motivated resistance movements to act against the Nazi regime and other totalitarian regimes, thereby doing a great service to justice and to humanity as a whole. For these people, it was indisputably evident that the law in force was actually unlawful. Yet when it comes to the decisions of a democratic politician, the question of what now corresponds to the law of truth, what is actually right and may be enacted as law, is less obvious. In terms of the underlying anthropological issues, what is right and may be given the force of law is in no way simply self-evident today. The question of how to recognize what is truly right and thus how to serve justice when framing laws has never been simple, and today in view of the vast extent of our knowledge and our capacity, it has become still harder.

How do we recognize what is right? In history, systems of law have almost always been based on religion: decisions regarding what was to be lawful among men were taken with reference to the divinity. Unlike other great religions, Christianity has never proposed a revealed law to the state and to society – that is to say, a juridical order derived from revelation. Instead, it has pointed to nature and reason as the true sources of law – and to the harmony of objective and subjective reason, which naturally presupposes that both spheres are rooted in the creative reason of God. Christian theologians thereby aligned themselves with a philosophical and juridical movement that began to take shape in the second century BC. In the first half of that century the social natural law developed by the Stoic philosophers came into contact with leading teachers of Roman law.[2] Through this encounter the juridical culture of the West was born, which was and is of key significance for the juridical culture of mankind. This pre-Christian marriage between law and philosophy opened up the path that led via the Christian Middle Ages and the juridical developments of the Age of Enlightenment all the way to the Declaration of Human Rights and to our German Basic Law of 1949, with which our nation committed itself to 'inviolable and inalienable human rights as the foundation of every human community, and of peace and justice in the world'.

For the development of law and for the development of humanity, it was highly significant that Christian theologians aligned themselves against the religious law associated with polytheism and on the side of philosophy, and that they acknowledged reason and nature in their interrelation as the universally valid source of law. This step had already been taken by St Paul in the Letter to the Romans, when he said: 'When Gentiles who have not the Law [the Torah of Israel] do by nature what the law requires, they are a law to themselves ... they show that what the law requires is written on their hearts, while their conscience also bears witness' (Rom. 2.14–15). Here we see the two fundamental concepts of nature and conscience, where conscience is nothing other than Solomon's listening heart, reason that is open to the language of being. If this seemed to offer a clear explanation of the foundations of legislation up to the time of the Enlightenment, up to the time of the Declaration on Human Rights after the Second World War and the framing of our Basic Law, there has been a dramatic shift in the situation in the last half-century. The idea of natural law is today viewed as a specifically Catholic doctrine, not worth bringing into the discussion in a non-Catholic environment, so that one feels almost ashamed even to mention the term.

Let me outline briefly how this situation arose. Fundamentally it is because of the idea that an unbridgeable gulf exists between 'is' and 'ought'.

An 'ought' can never follow from an 'is', because the two are situated on completely different planes. The reason for this is that, in the meantime, the positivist understanding of nature has come to be almost universally accepted. If nature – in the words of Hans Kelsen – is viewed as 'an aggregate of objective data linked together in terms of cause and effect', then indeed no ethical indication of any kind can be derived from it.[3] A positivist conception of nature as purely functional, as the natural sciences consider it to be, is incapable of producing any bridge to ethics and law, but once again yields only functional answers. The same also applies to reason, according to the positivist understanding which is widely held to be the only genuinely scientific one. Anything that is not verifiable or falsifiable, according to this understanding, does not belong to the realm of reason strictly understood. Hence ethics and religion must be assigned to the subjective field, and they remain extraneous to the realm of reason in the strict sense of the word. Where positivist reason dominates the field to the exclusion of all else – and that is broadly the case in our public mindset – then the classical sources of knowledge for ethics and law are excluded. This is a dramatic situation which affects everyone, and on which a public debate is necessary. Indeed, an essential goal of this address is to issue an urgent invitation to launch one.

The positivist approach to nature and reason, the positivist worldview in general, is a most important dimension of human knowledge and capacity that we may in no way dispense with. But in and of itself it is not a sufficient culture corresponding to the full breadth of the human condition. Where positivist reason considers itself the only sufficient culture and banishes all other cultural realities to the status of subcultures, it diminishes man; indeed it threatens his humanity. I say this with Europe specifically in mind, where there are concerted efforts to recognize only positivism as a common culture and a common basis for law-making, reducing all the other insights and values of our culture to the level of subculture, with the result that Europe vis-à-vis other world cultures is left in a state of culturelessness and, at the same time, extremist and radical movements emerge to fill the vacuum. In its self-proclaimed exclusivity, the positivist reason which recognizes nothing beyond mere functionality resembles a concrete bunker with no windows, in which we ourselves provide lighting and atmospheric conditions, being no longer willing to obtain either from God's wide world. And yet we cannot hide from ourselves the fact that, even in this artificial world, we are still covertly drawing on God's raw materials, which we refashion into our own products. The windows must be flung open again, we must see the wide world, the sky and the earth once more and learn to make proper use of all this.

But how are we to do this? How do we find our way out into the wide world, into the big picture? How can reason rediscover its true greatness, without being sidetracked into irrationality? How can nature reassert itself in its true depth, with all its demands, with all its directives? I would like to recall one of the developments in recent political history, hoping that I will neither be misunderstood nor provoke too many one-sided polemics. I would say that the emergence of the ecological movement in German politics since the 1970s, while it has not exactly flung open the windows, nevertheless was and continues to be a cry for fresh air which must not be ignored or pushed aside, just because too much of it is seen to be irrational. Young people had come to realize that something is wrong in our relationship with nature, that matter is not just raw material for us to shape at will, but that the earth has a dignity of its own and that we must follow its directives. In saying this, I am clearly not promoting any particular political party – nothing could be further from my mind. If something is wrong in our relationship with reality, then we must all reflect seriously on the whole situation and we are all prompted to question the very foundations of our culture.

Allow me to dwell a little longer on this point. The importance of ecology is no longer disputed. We must listen to the language of nature and we must respond accordingly. Yet I would like to underline a point that seems to me to be neglected, today as in the past: there is also an ecology of man. Man too has a nature that he must respect and that he cannot manipulate at will. Man is not merely self-creating freedom. Man does not create himself. He is intellect and will, but he is also nature, and his will is rightly ordered if he respects his nature, listens to it and accepts himself for who he is, as one who did not create himself. In this way, and in no other, is true human freedom fulfilled.

Let us come back to the fundamental concepts of nature and reason, from which we set out. The great proponent of legal positivism, Hans Kelsen, at the age of 84 – in 1965 – abandoned the dualism of 'is' and 'ought'. (I find it comforting that rational thought is evidently still possible at the age of 84!) Previously he had said that norms can only come from the will. Nature therefore could only contain norms, he adds, if a will had put them there. But this, he says, would presuppose a Creator God, whose will had entered into nature. 'Any attempt to discuss the truth of this belief is utterly futile,' he observed.[4] 'Is it really?', I find myself asking. Is it really pointless to wonder whether the objective reason that manifests itself in nature does not presuppose a creative reason, a *creator spiritus*?

At this point Europe's cultural heritage ought to come to our assistance. The conviction that there is a Creator God is what gave rise to the idea of human rights, the idea of the equality of all people before the law, the recognition of the inviolability of human dignity in every single person and the awareness of people's responsibility for their actions. Our cultural memory is shaped by these rational insights. To ignore it or dismiss it as a thing of the past would be to dismember our culture totally and to rob it of its completeness. The culture of Europe arose from the encounter between Jerusalem, Athens and Rome – from the encounter between Israel's monotheism, the philosophical reason of the Greeks and Roman law. This three-way encounter has shaped the inner identity of Europe. In the awareness of man's responsibility before God and in the acknowledgment of the inviolable dignity of every single human person it has established criteria of law: it is these criteria that we are called to defend at this moment in our history.

As he assumed the mantle of office, the young King Solomon was invited to make a request. How would it be if we, the lawmakers of today, were invited to make a request? What would we ask for? I think that, even today, there is ultimately nothing else we could wish for but a listening heart – the capacity to discern between good and evil, and thus to establish true law, to serve justice and peace. I thank you for your attention!

10

My Deep Thanks to God and to All of You

Benedict XVI
General Audience

St Peter's Square Wednesday,
27 February 2013

Venerable Brothers in the Episcopate and in the Presbyterate!
Distinguished Authorities!
Dear Brothers and Sisters!

I thank all of you for having come in such great numbers to this last General Audience. Heartfelt thanks! I am truly moved, and I see the Church alive! And I think we should also say thanks to the

Creator for the fine weather which he gives us, even on this winter day.

Like the Apostle Paul in the biblical text which we have heard, I too feel a deep need first and foremost to thank God, who gives guidance and growth to the Church, who sows his word and thus nourishes faith in his people. At this moment my heart expands and embraces the whole Church throughout the world; and I thank God for all that I have 'heard' in these years of the Petrine ministry about the faith in the Lord Jesus Christ and the love that truly circulates in the body of the Church and makes it live in love, and about the hope which opens and directs us towards the fullness of life, towards our heavenly homeland.

I feel that I bear everyone in prayer, in a present, God's present, in which I gather together every one of my meetings, journeys and pastoral visits. In prayer I gather each and all, in order to entrust them to the Lord: that we might be filled with the knowledge of his will, with all spiritual wisdom and understanding, and that we might lead a life worthy of him and of his love, bearing fruit in every good work (cf. Col. 1.9–10).

At this moment I feel great confidence, because I know, we all know, that the Gospel word of truth is the Church's strength; it is her life. The Gospel purifies and renews; it bears fruit, wherever the community of believers hears it and receives God's grace in truth and charity. This is my confidence; this is my joy.

When on 19 April nearly eight years ago I accepted the Petrine ministry, I had the firm certainty that has always accompanied me: this certainty of the life of the Church which comes from the word of God. At that moment, as I have often said, the words that echoed in my heart were: 'Lord, why are you asking this of me, and what is it that you are asking of me? It is a heavy burden which you are laying on my shoulders, but if you ask it of me, at your word I will cast the net, sure that you will lead me even with all my weaknesses.' And eight years later I can say that the Lord has truly led me; he has been close to me; I have been able to perceive his presence daily. It has been a portion of the Church's journey that has had its moments of joy and light, but also moments which were not easy. I have felt like St Peter with the Apostles in the boat on the Sea of Galilee: the Lord has given us so many days of sun and of light winds, days when the catch was abundant; there were also moments when the waters were rough and the winds against us, as throughout the Church's history, and the Lord seemed to be sleeping. But I have always known that the Lord is in that boat, and I have always known that the barque of the Church is not mine but his. Nor does the Lord let it sink; it is he who guides it, surely also through those whom he has chosen, because he so wished. This has been, and is, a certainty which nothing can shake. For this reason my heart today overflows with gratitude to God, for he has never let his Church, or me personally, lack his consolation, his light, his love.

We are in the Year of Faith which I desired precisely to reaffirm our faith in God in a context that seems to push him more and more into the background. I should like to invite all of us to renew our firm confidence in the Lord, to entrust ourselves like children to God's arms, certain that those arms always hold us, enabling us to press forward each day, even when the going gets tough. I want everyone to feel loved by that God who gave his Son for us and who has shown us his infinite love. I want everyone to feel the joy of being a Christian. In one beautiful morning prayer, it says: 'I adore you, my God, and I love you with all my heart. I thank you for having created me and made me a Christian.' Yes, we are happy for the gift of faith; it is our most precious possession, which no one can take from us! Let us thank the Lord for this daily, in prayer and by a consistent Christian life. God loves us, but he also expects us to love him!

But it is not only God whom I want to thank at this moment. The Pope is not alone in guiding the barque of Peter, even if it is his first responsibility. I have never felt alone in bearing the joy and the burden of the Petrine ministry; the Lord has set beside me so many people who, with generosity and love for God and the Church, have helped me and been close to me. Above all you, dear brother Cardinals: your wisdom, your counsel and your friendship have been invaluable to me; my co-workers, beginning with my Secretary of State who has faithfully accompanied me in these years; the Secretariat of State and the whole Roman Curia, as well as all those who in various sectors offer their service to the Holy See: many, many unseen faces that remain in the background, but who, precisely through their silent, daily dedication in a spirit of faith and humility, have been a sure and trustworthy support to me.

I also think in a special way of the Church of Rome, my diocese! I cannot forget my brothers in the episcopate and in the presbyterate, the consecrated persons and the entire people of God: in my pastoral visits, meetings, audiences and journeys I have always felt great kindness and deep affection. Yet I too have felt affection for each and all without distinction, with that pastoral charity which is the heart of every pastor, and especially of the bishop of Rome, the successor of the Apostle Peter. Every day I have borne each of you in prayer, with the heart of a father.

I would like my greeting and my thanksgiving to extend to everyone: the heart of the Pope reaches out to the whole world. And I wish to express my gratitude to the Diplomatic Corps accredited to the Holy See which represents the great family of the nations. Here I think too of all those who work for good communications, and I thank them for their important service.

At this point I would also like to thank most heartily all those people throughout the world who in these recent weeks have sent me moving expressions of concern, friendship and prayer. Yes, the Pope is never alone; now I once again experience this so overwhelmingly that my heart is touched. The Pope belongs to everyone and so many people feel very close to him. It is true that I receive letters from world leaders – from heads of state, from religious leaders, from representatives of the world of culture and so on. But I also receive many, many letters from ordinary people who write to me simply and from the heart, and who show me their affection, an affection born of our being together with Christ Jesus, in the Church. These people do not write to me in the way one writes, for example, to a prince or some important person they don't know. They write to me as brothers and sisters, as sons and daughters, with a sense of a very affectionate family bond.

Here one can sense palpably what the Church is – not an organization, an association for religious or humanitarian ends, but a living body, a communion of brothers and sisters in the Body of Christ, which makes us all one. To experience the Church in this way and to be able, as it were, to put one's finger on the strength of her truth and her love, is a cause for joy at a time when so many people are speaking of her decline. But we see how the Church is alive today!

In the last few months I have felt my energies declining, and I have asked God insistently in prayer to grant me his light and to help me make the right decision, not for my own good but for the good of the Church. I have taken this step with full awareness of its gravity and even its novelty, but with profound interior serenity. Loving the Church means also having the courage to make difficult, painful decisions, always looking to the good of the Church and not of oneself.

Here, allow me to go back once again to 19 April 2005. The real gravity of the decision was also due to the fact that from that moment on I was engaged always and for ever by the Lord. Always, anyone who accepts the Petrine ministry no longer has any privacy. He belongs always and completely to everyone, to the whole Church. In a manner of speaking, the private dimension of his life is completely eliminated. I was able to experience, and I experience even now, the fact that one receives one's life precisely when one gives it away. Earlier I said that many people who love the Lord also love the successor of St Peter and feel great affection for him; that the Pope truly has brothers and sisters, sons and daughters, throughout the world, and that he feels secure in the embrace of your communion; because he no longer belongs to himself, he belongs to all and all belong to him.

The 'always' is also a 'for ever' – there can no longer be a return to the private sphere. My decision to resign the active exercise of the ministry does not revoke this. I do not return to private life, to a life of travel, meetings, receptions, conferences and so on. I am not abandoning the Cross, but remaining in a new way at the side of the crucified Lord. I no longer bear the power of office for the governance of the Church, but in the service of prayer I remain, so to speak, in the enclosure of St Peter. St Benedict, whose name I bear as Pope, will be a great example for me in this. He showed us the way for a life which, whether active or passive, is completely given over to the work of God.

I also thank each and every one of you for the respect and understanding with which you have accepted this important decision. I will continue to accompany the Church's journey with prayer and reflection, with that devotion to the Lord and his bride which I have hitherto sought to practise daily and which I would like to practise always. I ask you to remember me in prayer before God, and above all to pray for the cardinals, who are called to so weighty a task, and for the new successor of the Apostle Peter: may the Lord accompany him with the light and strength of his Spirit.

Let us call upon the maternal intercession of the Virgin Mary, Mother of God and Mother of the Church, that she may accompany each of us and the whole ecclesial community; to her let us commend ourselves with deep confidence.

Dear friends! God guides his Church; he sustains it always, especially at times of difficulty. Let us never lose this vision of faith, which is the one true way of looking at the journey of the Church and of the world. In our hearts, in the heart of each of you, may there always abide the joyful certainty that the Lord is at our side: he does not abandon us, he remains close to us and he surrounds us with his love. Thank you!

Appendix

Pastoral Letter to the People of Ireland

Dear brothers and sisters of the Church in Ireland, it is with great concern that I write to you as pastor of the universal Church. Like yourselves, I have been deeply disturbed by the information that has come to light regarding the abuse of children and vulnerable young people by members of the Church in Ireland, particularly by priests and religious. I can only share in the dismay and the sense of betrayal that so many of you have experienced on learning of these sinful and criminal acts and the way Church authorities in Ireland dealt with them.

As you know, I recently invited the Irish bishops to a meeting here in Rome to give an account of their handling of these matters in the past and to outline the steps they have taken to respond to this grave situation. Together with senior officials of the Roman Curia, I listened to what they had to say, both individually and as a group, as they offered an analysis of mistakes made and lessons learned, and a description of the programmes and protocols now in place. Our discussions were frank and constructive. I am confident that, as a result, the bishops will now be in a stronger position to carry forward the work of repairing past injustices and confronting the broader issues associated with the abuse of minors in a way consonant with the demands of justice and the teachings of the Gospel.

For my part, considering the gravity of these offences, and the often inadequate response to them on the part of the ecclesiastical authorities in your country, I have decided to write this Pastoral Letter to express my closeness to you and to propose a path of healing, renewal and reparation.

It is true, as many in your country have pointed out, that the problem of child abuse is peculiar neither to Ireland nor to the Church. Nevertheless, the task you now face is to address the problem of abuse that has occurred within the Irish Catholic community, and to do so with courage and determination. No one imagines that this painful situation will be resolved swiftly. Real progress has been made, yet much more remains to be done. Perseverance and prayer are needed, with great trust in the healing power of God's grace.

At the same time, I must also express my conviction that, in order to recover from this grievous wound, the Church in Ireland must first acknowledge before the Lord and before others the serious sins committed against defenceless children. Such an acknowledgement, accompanied by sincere sorrow for the damage caused to these victims and their families, must lead to a concerted effort to ensure the protection of children from similar crimes in the future.

As you take up the challenges of this hour, I ask you to remember 'the rock from which you were hewn' (Is. 51.1). Reflect on the generous, often heroic, contributions made by past generations of Irish men and women to the Church and to humanity as a whole, and let this provide the impetus for honest self-examination and a committed programme of ecclesial and individual renewal. It is my prayer that, assisted by the intercession of her many saints and purified through penance, the Church in Ireland will overcome the present crisis and become once more a convincing witness to the truth and the goodness of Almighty God, made manifest in his Son Jesus Christ.

Historically, the Catholics of Ireland have proved an enormous force for good at home and abroad. Celtic monks like St Columbanus spread the Gospel in western Europe and laid the foundations of medieval monastic culture. The ideals of holiness, charity and transcendent wisdom born of the Christian faith found expression in the building of churches and monasteries and the establishment of schools, libraries and hospitals, all of which helped to consolidate the spiritual identity of Europe. Those Irish missionaries drew their strength and inspiration from the firm faith, strong leadership and upright morals of the Church in their native land.

From the sixteenth century on, Catholics in Ireland endured a long period of persecution, during which they struggled to keep the flame of faith alive in dangerous and difficult circumstances. St Oliver Plunkett, the martyred archbishop of Armagh, is the most famous example of a host of courageous sons and daughters of Ireland who were willing to lay down their lives out of fidelity to the Gospel. After Catholic emancipation, the Church was free to grow once more. Families and countless individuals who had preserved the faith in times of trial became the catalyst for the great resurgence of Irish Catholicism in the nineteenth century. The Church provided education, especially for the poor, and this was to make a major contribution to Irish society.

Among the fruits of the new Catholic schools was a rise in vocations: generations of missionary priests, sisters and brothers left their homeland to serve in every continent, especially in the English-speaking world. They were remarkable not only for their great numbers but also for the strength of their faith and the steadfastness of their pastoral commitment. Many dioceses, especially in Africa, America and Australia, benefited from the presence of Irish clergy and religious who preached the Gospel and established parishes, schools and universities, clinics and hospitals that served both Catholics and the community at large, with particular attention to the needs of the poor.

In almost every family in Ireland there has been someone – a son or a daughter, an aunt or an uncle – who has given his or her life to the Church. Irish families rightly esteem and cherish their loved ones who have dedicated their lives to Christ, sharing the gift of faith with others, and putting that faith into action in loving service of God and neighbour.

In recent decades, however, the Church in your country has had to confront new and serious challenges to the faith arising from the rapid transformation and secularization of Irish society. Fast-paced social change has occurred, often adversely affecting people's traditional adherence to Catholic teaching and values. All too often the sacramental and devotional practices that sustain faith and enable it to grow, such as frequent confession, daily prayer and annual retreats, were neglected. Significant too was the tendency during this period, also on the part of priests and religious, to adopt ways of thinking and assessing secular realities without sufficient reference to the Gospel. The programme of renewal proposed by the Second Vatican Council was sometimes misinterpreted and indeed, in the light of the profound social changes that were taking place, it was far from easy to know how best to implement it. In particular, there was a well-intentioned but misguided tendency to avoid penal approaches to canonically irregular situations. It is in this overall context that we must try to understand the disturbing problem of child sexual abuse, which has contributed in no small measure to the weakening of faith and the loss of respect for the Church and her teachings.

Only by examining carefully the many elements that gave rise to the present crisis can a clear-sighted diagnosis of its causes be undertaken and effective remedies be found. Certainly, among the contributing factors we can include: inadequate procedures for determining the suitability of candidates for the priesthood and the religious life; insufficient human, moral, intellectual and spiritual formation in seminaries and novitiates; a tendency in society to favour the clergy and other authority figures; and a misplaced concern for the reputation of the Church and the avoidance of scandal, resulting in failure to apply existing canonical penalties and to safeguard the dignity of every person. Urgent action is needed to address these factors, which have had such tragic consequences in the lives of victims and their families, and have obscured the light of the Gospel to a degree that not even centuries of persecution succeeded in doing.

On several occasions since my election to the See of Peter, I have met with victims of sexual abuse, as indeed I am ready to do in the future. I have sat with them, I have listened to their stories, I have acknowledged their suffering and I have prayed with them and for them. Earlier in my pontificate, in my concern to address this matter, I asked the bishops of Ireland, 'to establish the truth of what happened in the past, to take whatever steps are necessary to prevent it from occurring again, to ensure that the principles of justice are fully respected, and above all, to bring healing to the victims and to all those affected by these egregious crimes'.[1]

With this letter I wish to exhort *all of you,* as God's people in Ireland, to reflect on the wounds inflicted on Christ's body, the sometimes painful remedies needed to bind and heal them, and the need for unity, charity and mutual support in the long-term process of restoration and ecclesial renewal. I now turn to you with words that come from my heart, and I wish to speak to each of you individually and to all of you as brothers and sisters in the Lord.

To the victims of abuse and their families I say, you have suffered grievously and I am truly sorry. I know that nothing can undo the wrong you have endured. Your trust has been betrayed, and your dignity has been violated. Many of you found that, when you were courageous enough to speak of what happened to you, no one would listen. Those of you who were abused in residential institutions must have felt that there was no escape from your sufferings. It is understandable that you find it hard to forgive or be reconciled with the Church. In her name, I openly express the shame and remorse that we all feel. At the same time, I ask you not to lose hope. It is in the communion of the Church that we encounter the person of Jesus Christ, who was himself a victim of injustice and sin. Like you, he still bears the wounds of his own unjust suffering. He understands the depths of your pain and its enduring effect upon your lives and your relationships, including your relationship with the Church. I know some of you find it difficult even to enter the doors of a church after all that has occurred. Yet Christ's own wounds, transformed by his redemptive sufferings, are the very means by which the power of evil is broken and we are reborn to life and hope. I believe deeply in the healing power of his self-sacrificing love – even in the darkest and most hopeless situations – to bring liberation and the promise of a new beginning.

Speaking to you as a pastor concerned for the good of all God's children, I humbly ask you to consider what I have said. I pray that, by drawing nearer to Christ and by participating in the life of his Church – a Church purified by penance and renewed in pastoral charity – you will come to rediscover Christ's infinite love for each one of you. I am confident that in this way you will be able to find reconciliation, deep inner healing and peace.

To priests and religious who have abused children, I say you betrayed the trust that was placed in you by innocent young people and their parents, and you must answer for it before Almighty God and before properly constituted tribunals. You have forfeited the esteem of the people of Ireland and brought shame and dishonour upon your confrères. Those of you who are priests violated the sanctity of the sacrament of Holy Orders in which Christ makes himself present in us and in our actions. Together with the immense harm done to victims, great damage has been done to the Church and to the public perception of the priesthood and religious life.

I urge you to examine your conscience, take responsibility for the sins you have committed and humbly express your sorrow. Sincere repentance opens the door to God's forgiveness and the grace of true amendment. By offering prayers and penance for those you have wronged, you should seek to atone personally for your actions. Christ's redeeming sacrifice has the power to forgive even the gravest of sins, and to bring forth good from even the most terrible evil. At the same time, God's justice summons us to give an account of our actions and to conceal nothing. Openly acknowledge your guilt, submit yourselves to the demands of justice, but do not despair of God's mercy.

To parents, I say you have been deeply shocked to learn of the terrible things that took place in what ought to be the safest and most secure environment of all. In today's world it is not easy to build a home and to bring up children. They deserve to grow up in security, loved and cherished, with a strong sense of their identity and worth.

They have a right to be educated in authentic moral values rooted in the dignity of the human person, to be inspired by the truth of our Catholic faith and to learn ways of behaving and acting that lead to healthy self-esteem and lasting happiness. This noble but demanding task is entrusted in the first place to you, their parents. I urge you to play your part in ensuring the best possible care of children, both at home and in society as a whole, while the Church, for her part, continues to implement the measures adopted in recent years to protect young people in parish and school environments. As you carry out your vital responsibilities, be assured that I remain close to you and I offer you the support of my prayers.

To the children and young people of Ireland, I say that I wish to offer you a particular word of encouragement. Your experience of the Church is very different from that of your parents and grandparents. The world has changed greatly since they were your age. Yet all people, in every generation, are called to travel the same path through life, whatever their circumstances may be. We are all scandalized by the sins and failures of some of the Church's members, particularly those who were chosen especially to guide and serve young people. But it is *in the Church* that you will find Jesus Christ, who is the same yesterday, today and for ever (cf. Heb. 13.8). He loves you and he has offered himself on the cross for you. Seek a personal relationship with him within the communion of his Church, for he will never betray your trust! He alone can satisfy your deepest longings and give your lives their fullest meaning by directing them to the service of others. Keep your eyes fixed on Jesus and his goodness, and shelter the flame of faith in your heart. Together with your fellow Catholics in Ireland, I look to you to be faithful disciples of our Lord and to bring your much-needed enthusiasm and idealism to the rebuilding and renewal of our beloved Church.

To the priests and religious of Ireland, I say all of us are suffering as a result of the sins of our confrères who betrayed a sacred trust or failed to deal justly and responsibly with allegations of abuse. In view of the outrage and indignation that this has provoked, not only among the lay faithful but among yourselves and your religious communities, many of you feel personally discouraged, even abandoned. I am also aware that in some people's eyes you are tainted by association, and viewed as if you were somehow responsible for the misdeeds of others. At this painful time I want to acknowledge the dedication of your priestly and religious lives and apostolates, and I invite you to reaffirm your faith in Christ, your love of his Church and your confidence in the Gospel's promise of redemption, forgiveness and interior renewal. In this way, you will demonstrate for all to see that where sin abounds, grace abounds all the more (cf. Rom. 5.20).

I know that many of you are disappointed, bewildered and angered by the way these matters have been handled by some of your superiors. Yet it is essential that you cooperate closely with those in authority and help to ensure that the measures adopted to respond to the crisis will be truly evangelical, just and effective. Above all, I urge you to become ever more clearly men and women of prayer, courageously following the path of conversion, purification and reconciliation. In this way, the Church in Ireland will draw new life and vitality from your witness to the Lord's redeeming power made visible in your lives.

To my brother bishops I say it cannot be denied that some of you and your predecessors failed, at times grievously, to apply the long-established norms of canon law to the crime of child abuse. Serious mistakes were made in responding to allegations. I recognize how difficult it was to grasp the extent and complexity of the problem, to obtain reliable information and to make the right decisions in the light of conflicting expert advice.

Nevertheless, it must be admitted that grave errors of judgement were made and failures of leadership occurred. All this has seriously undermined your credibility and effectiveness. I appreciate the efforts you have made to remedy past mistakes and to guarantee that they do not happen again. Besides fully implementing the norms of canon law in addressing cases of child abuse, continue to cooperate with the civil authorities in their area of competence.

Clearly, religious superiors should do likewise. They too have taken part in recent discussions here in Rome with a view to establishing a clear and consistent approach to these matters. It is imperative that the child safety norms of the Church in Ireland be continually revised and updated and that they be applied fully and impartially in conformity with canon law.

Only decisive action carried out with complete honesty and transparency will restore the respect and good will of the Irish people towards the Church to which we have consecrated our lives. This must arise, first and foremost, from your own self-examination, inner purification and spiritual renewal. The Irish people rightly expect you to be men of God, to be holy, to live simply, to pursue personal conversion daily. For them, in the words of St Augustine, you are a bishop;

yet with them you are called to be a follower of Christ (cf. Sermon 340, 1). I therefore exhort you to renew your sense of accountability before God, to grow in solidarity with your people and to deepen your pastoral concern for all the members of your flock. In particular, I ask you to be attentive to the spiritual and moral lives of each one of your priests. Set them an example by your own lives, be close to them, listen to their concerns, offer them encouragement at this difficult time and stir up the flame of their love for Christ and their commitment to the service of their brothers and sisters.

The lay faithful, too, should be encouraged to play their proper part in the life of the Church. See that they are formed in such a way that they can offer an articulate and convincing account of the Gospel in the midst of modern society (cf. 1 Pet. 3.15) and cooperate more fully in the Church's life and mission. This in turn will help you once again become credible leaders and witnesses to the redeeming truth of Christ.

To all the faithful of Ireland I say a young person's experience of the Church should always bear fruit in a personal and life-giving encounter with Jesus Christ within a loving, nourishing community. In this environment young people should be encouraged to grow to their full human and spiritual stature, to aspire to high ideals of holiness, charity and truth, and to draw inspiration from the riches of a great religious and cultural tradition. In our increasingly secularized society, where even we Christians often find it difficult to speak of the transcendent dimension of our existence, we need to find new ways to pass on to young people the beauty and richness of friendship with Jesus Christ in the communion of his Church. In confronting the present crisis, measures to deal justly with individual crimes are essential, yet on their own they are not enough: a new vision is needed, to inspire present and future generations to treasure the gift of our common faith. By treading the path marked out by the Gospel, by observing the commandments and by conforming your lives ever more closely to the figure of Jesus Christ, you will surely experience the profound renewal that is so urgently needed at this time. I invite you all to persevere along this path.

Dear brothers and sisters in Christ, it is out of deep concern for all of you at this painful time, in which the fragility of the human condition has been so starkly revealed, that I have wished to offer these words of encouragement and support. I hope that you will receive them as a sign of my spiritual closeness and my confidence in your ability to respond to the challenges of the present hour by drawing renewed inspiration and strength from Ireland's noble traditions of fidelity to the Gospel, perseverance in the faith and steadfastness in the pursuit of holiness. In solidarity with all of you, I am praying earnestly that, by God's grace, the wounds afflicting so many individuals and families may be healed and that the Church in Ireland may experience a season of rebirth and spiritual renewal.

I now wish to propose to you some concrete initiatives to address the situation. At the conclusion of my meeting with the Irish bishops, I asked that Lent this year be set aside as a time to pray for an outpouring of God's mercy and the Holy Spirit's gifts of holiness and strength upon the Church in your country. I now invite all of you to devote your Friday penances, for a period of one year, between now and Easter 2011, to this intention. I ask you to offer up your fasting, your prayer, your reading of Scripture and your works of mercy in order to obtain the grace of healing and renewal for the Church in Ireland. I encourage you to discover anew the sacrament of Reconciliation and to avail yourselves more frequently of the transforming power of its grace.

Particular attention should also be given to Eucharistic adoration, and in every diocese there should be churches or chapels specifically devoted to this purpose. I ask parishes, seminaries, religious houses and monasteries to organize periods of Eucharistic adoration, so that all have an opportunity to take part. Through intense prayer before the real presence of the Lord, you can make reparation for the sins of abuse that have done so much harm, at the same time imploring the grace of renewed strength and a deeper sense of mission on the part of all bishops, priests, religious and lay faithful.

I am confident that this programme will lead to a rebirth of the Church in Ireland in the fullness of God's own truth, for it is the truth that sets us free (cf. Jn 8.32).

Furthermore, having consulted and prayed about the matter, I intend to hold an Apostolic Visitation of certain dioceses in Ireland, as well as seminaries and religious congregations. Arrangements for the Visitation, which is intended to assist the local Church on her path of renewal, will be made in cooperation with the competent offices of the Roman Curia and the Irish Episcopal Conference. The details will be announced in due course.

I also propose that a nationwide Mission be held for all bishops, priests and religious. It is my hope that, by drawing on the expertise of experienced preachers and retreat-givers from Ireland and from elsewhere, and by exploring anew the conciliar documents, the liturgical rites of ordination and profession, and recent pontifical teaching, you will come to a more profound appreciation of your respective vocations, so as to rediscover the roots of your faith in Jesus Christ and to drink deeply from the springs of living water that he offers you through his Church.

In this Year for Priests I commend to you most particularly the figure of St John Mary Vianney, who had such a rich understanding of the mystery of the priesthood. 'The priest,' he wrote, 'holds the key to the treasures of heaven: it is he who opens the door: he is the steward of the good Lord; the administrator of his goods.' The Curé d'Ars understood well how greatly blessed a community is when served by a good and holy priest: 'A good shepherd, a pastor after God's heart, is the greatest treasure which the good Lord can grant to a parish, and one of the most precious gifts of divine mercy.' Through the intercession of St John Mary Vianney, may the priesthood in Ireland be revitalized, and may the whole Church in Ireland grow in appreciation for the great gift of the priestly ministry.

I take this opportunity to thank in anticipation all those who will be involved in the work of organizing the Apostolic Visitation and the Mission, as well as the many men and women throughout Ireland already working for the safety of children in church environments. Since the time when the gravity and extent of the problem of child sexual abuse in Catholic institutions first began to be fully grasped, the Church has done an immense amount of work in many parts of the world in order to address and remedy it. While no effort should be spared in improving and updating existing procedures, I am encouraged by the fact that the current safeguarding practices adopted by local Churches are being seen, in some parts of the world, as a model for other institutions to follow.

I wish to conclude this Letter with a special Prayer for the Church in Ireland, which I send to you with the care of a father for his children and with the affection of a fellow Christian, scandalized and hurt by what has occurred in our beloved Church. As you make use of this prayer in your families, parishes and communities, may the Blessed Virgin Mary protect and guide each of you to a closer union with her Son, crucified and risen. With great affection and unswerving confidence in God's promises, I cordially impart to all of you my Apostolic Blessing as a pledge of strength and peace in the Lord.

*From the Vatican, 19 March 2010, on the
Solemnity of St Joseph*

BENEDICTUS PP. XVI

Prayer for the Church in Ireland

God of our fathers,

renew us in the faith which is our life and salvation,

the hope which promises forgiveness and interior renewal,

the charity which purifies and opens our hearts

to love you, and in you, each of our brothers and sisters.

Lord Jesus Christ,

may the Church in Ireland renew her age-old commitment

to the education of our young people in the way of truth and goodness, holiness and generous service to society.

Holy Spirit, comforter, advocate and guide,

inspire a new springtime of holiness and apostolic zeal

for the Church in Ireland.

May our sorrow and our tears,

our sincere effort to redress past wrongs,

and our firm purpose of amendment

bear an abundant harvest of grace
for the deepening of the faith
in our families, parishes, schools and communities,
for the spiritual progress of Irish society,
and the growth of charity, justice, joy and peace
within the whole human family.
To you, Triune God,
confident in the loving protection of Mary,
Queen of Ireland, our Mother,
and of St Patrick, St Brigid and all the saints,
do we entrust ourselves, our children,
and the needs of the Church in Ireland.
Amen.

Notes

CHAPTER 2

1 John Paul II, *Memory and Identity*, London:
Weidenfeld and Nicolson, 2005, p. 189.
2 John Paul II, *Memory and Identity*, pp. 189ff.
3 Walter M. Abbott SJ, *The Documents of Vatican II*,
London: Geoffrey Chapman, 1966, p. 715.
4 Cf. Abbott, *The Documents of Vatican II*, p. 715.

CHAPTER 5

1 Of the total number of 26 conversations (διάλεξις
– Khoury translates this as 'controversy') in the
dialogue ('Entretien'), Theodore Khoury published
the seventh 'controversy' with footnotes and an
extensive introduction on the origin of the text,
on the manuscript tradition and on the structure
of the dialogue, together with brief summaries
of the 'controversies' not included in the edition.
The Greek text is accompanied by a French
translation: 'Manuel II Paléologue, Entretiens avec
un Musulman. 7ᵉ Controverse', *Sources Chrétiennes*
115, Paris, 1966. In the meantime, Karl Förstel

published in *Corpus Islamico-Christianum* (*Series Graeca*, ed. A. T. Khoury and R. Glei) an edition of the text in Greek and German with commentary: *Manuel II. Palaiologus: Dialoge mit einem Muslim*, 3 vols, Würzburg-Altenberge, 1993–6. As early as 1966, E. Trapp had published the Greek text with an introduction as vol. II of *Wiener byzantinische Studien*. I shall be quoting from Khoury's edition.

2   On the origin and redaction of the dialogue, cf. Khoury, 'Manuel II Paléologue, Entretiens avec un Musulman', pp. 22–9; extensive comments in this regard can also be found in the editions of Förstel and Trapp.

3   Controversy VII, 2 c: Khoury, 'Manuel II Paléologue, Entretiens avec un Musulman', pp. 142–3; Förstel, *Manuel II. Palaiologus: Dialoge mit einem Muslim*, vol. I, VII, Dialog 1.5, pp. 240–1. In the Muslim world this quotation has unfortunately been taken as an expression of my personal position, thus arousing understandable indignation. I hope that the reader of my text can see immediately that this sentence does not express my personal view of the Qur'an, for which I have the respect due to the holy book of a great religion. In quoting the text of the Emperor Manuel II, I intended solely to draw out the essential relationship between faith and reason. On this point I am in agreement with Manuel II, but without endorsing his polemic.

4   Controversy VII, 3 b–c: Khoury, 'Manuel II Paléologue, Entretiens avec un Musulman', pp. 144–5; Förstel, *Manuel II. Palaiologus: Dialoge mit einem Muslim*, vol. I, VII, Dialog 1.6, pp. 240–3.

5 It was purely for the sake of this statement that
   I quoted the dialogue between Manuel and his
   Persian interlocutor. In this statement the theme of
   my subsequent reflections emerges.

6 Cf. Khoury, 'Manuel II Paléologue, Entretiens avec
   un Musulman', p. 144, n. 1.

7 R. Arnaldez, *Grammaire et théologie chez Ibn Hazm
   de Cordoue*, Paris, 1956, p. 13; cf. Khoury, 'Manuel
   II Paléologue, Entretiens avec un Musulman',
   p. 144. The fact that comparable positions exist in
   the theology of the late Middle Ages will appear
   later in my discourse.

8 Regarding the widely discussed interpretation
   of the episode of the burning bush, I refer to
   my book *Introduction to Christianity,* London,
   1969, pp. 77–93 (originally published in
   German as *Einführung in das Christentum,*
   Munich, 1968 [NB The pages quoted refer to
   the entire chapter entitled 'The Biblical Belief in
   God']). I think that my statements in that book,
   despite later developments in the discussion,
   remain valid today.

9 Cf. A. Schenker, 'L'Écriture sainte subsiste
   en plusieurs formes canoniques simultanées',
   in *L'Interpretazione della Bibbia nella Chiesa.
   Atti del Simposio promosso dalla Congregazione
   per la Dottrina della Fede*, Vatican City, 2001,
   pp. 178–86.

10 On this matter I expressed myself in greater detail
   in my book *The Spirit of the Liturgy*, San Francisco,
   2000, pp. 44–50.

11 Of the vast literature on the theme of de-
   Hellenization, I would like to mention above all
   A. Grillmeier, 'Hellenisierung-Judaisierung des

Christentums als Deuteprinzipien der Geschichte des kirchlichen Dogmas', in A. Grillmeier, *Mit ihm und in ihm. Christologische Forschungen und Perspektiven*, Freiburg, 1975, pp. 423–88.

12 Newly published with commentary by Heino Sonnemans (ed.): *Joseph Ratzinger-Benedikt XVI, Der Gott des Glaubens und der Gott der Philosophen. Ein Beitrag zum Problem der theologia naturalis*, Leutesdorf: Johannes-Verlag, 2nd rev. edn, 2005.

13 Cf. 90 c–d. For this text, cf. also R. Guardini, *Der Tod des Sokrates*, 5th edn, Mainz-Paderborn, 1987, pp. 218–21.

CHAPTER 6

1 Jean LeClercq, *Le Jour de l'homme*, Paris: Éditions du Seuil, 1976, p. 35.

2 LeClercq, *Le Jour de l'homme*, p. 21.

3 LeClercq, *Le Jour de l'homme*, p. 229.

CHAPTER 8

1 *L'Osservatore Romano*, 19 September 2010, p. 4.

CHAPTER 9

1 *Contra Celsum*, Book 1, Chapter 1. Cf. A. Fürst, 'Monotheismus und Monarchie: zum Zusammenhang von Heil und Herrschaft in der Antike', *Theological Philosophy* 81 (2006), pp. 321–38, quoted on p. 336; cf. also J. Ratzinger, *Die Einheit der Nationen. Eine Vision der Kirchenväter*, Salzburg and Munich, 1971, p. 60.

2   Cf. W. Waldstein, *Ins Herz geschrieben: das Naturrecht als Fundament einer menschlichen Gesellschaft* (Augsburg, 2010), pp. 11ff., 31–61.

3   Cf. Waldstein, *Ins Herz geschrieben*, pp. 15–21.

4   Cf. Waldstein, *Ins Herz geschrieben*, p. 19.

APPENDIX

1   Address to the Bishops of Ireland, 28 October 2006.